Stephen L. Gruneberg
David H. Weight

Feasibility Studies in Construction

Mitchell·London

First published 1990

Typeset by Latimer Trend & Company Ltd, Plymouth
and printed in Great Britain by Courier International Ltd,
Tiptree, Essex.

Published by The Mitchell Publishing Company Limited
4 Fitzhardinge Street, London W1H 0AH
A subsidiary of B T Batsford Limited

A CIP catalogue record for this book is
available from the British Library

ISBN 0 7134 5964 6

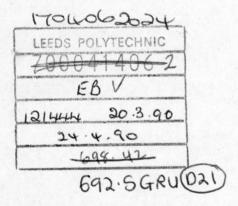

contents

Preface

PART I

Contents

preface

This book is in three parts. The *first part* introduces some of the general concepts and techniques of studying the feasibility of construction projects. The *second part* suggests a computer application, which uses a common sense approach to costing, and the *third part* develops the idea of teamwork by considering the problem of studying feasibility from various points of view.

It is hoped that this book may contribute towards a discussion of the application of computers and the development of teamwork in the construction industry. If it stimulates discussion about the need for closer working relationships within the industry between the professions and contractors and if it encourages the use of computer techniques and information technology in the building industry, it will have more than succeeded in its objectives.

This book is aimed at all professional groups currently working in the construction industry as well as those wishing to enter it as managers and designers. The book should therefore appeal to those studying quantity surveying, civil and structural engineering, architecture and construction management at HND, degree and post graduate levels. Students sitting professional examinations should also find the book useful. Hopefully there is something in it for everyone in the industry. Moreover, parts of the book should be of use to those not directly involved in the construction process, including the client, lawyers, planners and financial advisors.

This book has been the result of many late nights and long meetings depriving families and friends of the time and consideration they deserve. For their understanding, help and patience the authors are truly grateful, especially to Elizabeth and Jan. Sincere thanks are also due to Thelma Nye, Tony Seward and Paul Bolton, who have been marvellous to work with on this project. Their work, kindness and encouragement have greatly lightened the burden of writing this book.

London and Poole 1990   *SLG and DW*

PART I

one

The background to feasibility studies

Introduction

A feasibility study is often the starting point of a rational decision making process. There is a need to understand the nature and implications of management decisions. Above all, there is a need to help management make better decisions. Feasibility studies attempt to meet this demand, which arises out of the requirement to communicate decisions or recommendations and their potential consequences to clients, various members of the building team, local planning authorities and other interested parties. A systematic approach to assist in making comparisons between options is supported by a body of economic theory.

Exponents of this theory recognise its limitations, and it is only by appreciating some of these limitations that the methods of studying the viability of proposals can best be applied. One limitation of the theory is that it does not help to initiate options, only to develop them. Another limitation is that because the results of a feasibility study are deduced from a set of assumptions, the feasibility study will only be as good or as bad as these assumptions, which may often be inaccurate, arbitrary or unmeasurable. There are therefore severe restrictions on the blind acceptance of the results of studies, but various techniques and forms of argument have been devised to overcome some of these objections. In the public arena of planning appeals, these techniques can be used equally by those in favour or against given proposals.

This chapter will examine some of the theoretical background to decision making theory, define various techniques and place these modern approaches in an historical perspective to show that the techniques are relatively new and much work remains to be done to refine and improve them. Nevertheless, the methods discussed in the rest of this book will show that feasibility studies are useful for planning, budgeting and design purposes as well as helping building clients to obtain planning permission and inform the general public of intentions. While they inform the client of the likely cost of a project, they are still capable of taking environmental issues into account.

Definition of feasibility

The Concise Oxford Dictionary definition of the term 'feasible' is 'practicable, possible; (loosely) manageable, convenient, serviceable, plausible'. Feasibility studies examine proposals in order to establish the degree to which these attributes, amongst others, are present. A project should be *practicable* in that the financial resources should be available; *manageable* in so far as the management skills and experience are present, and *serviceable* in the sense that the proposal is understood in all its aspects to permit it to function as planned. *A feasibility study is a report designed to highlight, evaluate and structure the advantages and disadvantages over time of alternative solutions to given problems.* The outcome of a feasibility study should be a set of qualified recommendations based on explicit mathematical decision criteria or reasoned argument or a combination of both.

Historic background

It is possible to trace the modern systematic approach of feasibility studies back to the Enlightenment and the Age of Reason, around the turn of the eighteenth century, when a separation of the ideas of theology and the secular state took place. People could hold critical views without necessarily incurring the wrath of the State and Church. According to ROGERS, from the period of the Enlightenment emerged 'the doctrines of the right of private judgement, of universal equality, of government as a police power and nothing more'.[1] These are all necessary requirements of the approach to feasibility studies adopted in this book.

The separation of roles of Church and State opened the way for COMTE HENRI DE SAINT-SIMON (1760–1825), who was active during the earlier stages of the French Revolution, and AUGUSTE COMTE (1798–1857) to develop Positivism in which the positive spirit of the sciences of mathematics, physics and chemistry could be applied to the human condition to understand, manipulate and improve society. The political will existed in Europe, especially in France leading up to and following the Revolution of 1789, to 'extend the benefits of civilisation to those classes which had hitherto had little share in them.[2]

ROGERS argues that the ideas of Positivism go back to the Middle Ages, before the period of the Enlightenment and its individualistic dogmas. 'Like the Middle Ages (Positivism) insists upon the need for an independent spiritual power to formulate the doctrines on which society is found and morality based. But these doctrines are no longer theological; they are the outcome of science.'[3] To SAINT-SIMON there was a common purpose, for which members of society strove, and, given a proper understanding of this aim, scientific methods could be found how best to achieve them. The Positivist approach therefore involved scientific method as a means of dealing with social issues. 'COMTE believed that human society itself could be investigated and regulated according to scientific method.'[4] There is, however, at least one major objection to the Positivists, as PLAMENATZ points out in discussing SAINT-SIMON: 'Why, if there is to be moral order, if there is to be no serious disagreements about the right and the desirable, no adherence to values which are seriously incompatible, need there be a pre-eminant purpose shared by everyone? Where has there ever been such a purpose, except in times of war?'[5]

Nevertheless, in the first half of the nineteenth century, while HIPPO-LYTE TAINE extended Positivism to psychology, history and art, JULES DUPUIT, the French economist and engineer, extended it to economics in his book *On the Measure of Utility of Public Works* published in 1844, eight years before COMTE's own book, *Catechisme Positiviste*. According to MERKHOFER, DUPUIT was the intellectual father of cost benefit theory. Cost benefit studies, MERKHOFER asserts, 'emerged from applications of economic theory originally conducted in the late nineteenth century directed at evaluating proposals for the construction of waste-paper disposal systems'.[6] A systematic approach to dealing with social problems by applying economic concepts and scientific methodology had thus been established, at least in the United States, by the beginning of this century.

Systematic techniques continue to be developed in applications in the construction industry to evaluate and plan building projects. However, until the early years of the nineteenth century, buildings had been erected without a clear budget. In Great Britain, as the construction of a building progressed, drawings and specifications were produced and labour and materials were measured and costed against these documents, without the client knowing what the final total cost would be. This arrangement was called a *Measure and Value Contract* and proved most unsatisfactory when the excessive costs of building Buckingham Palace and Windsor Palace became known. From the middle of the nineteenth century, Contracts in Gross were used to provide estimates in advance. Contractors then took on the responsibility of constructing the building within the estimate, which they themselves had quoted prior to appointment.

In America one of the first applications of cost benefit analysis was the assessment of the costs and benefits of all river and harbour developments as a result of the River and Harbor Act of 1902, which directed the Corps of Engineers to carry out studies of projects. In the UK the first major feasibility study, since the Second World War, was undertaken in 1960 by COBURN, BEESLEY and REYNOLDS to evaluate the proposal to build the M1 motorway. Since then there have been many studies, including a major transport study to evaluate the Victoria Line on London's Underground and the ROSKILL Commission of 1970, which examined the proposal for a third airport for London. Many other studies have been carried out as a matter of routine in factories and offices whenever projects or proposals require economic evaluations.

Economic background

Because resources are scarce, it is always necessary to choose between options. Even in situations where resources appear to be abundant, opportunities will present themselves and choices must be made. This problem of choice is referred to by economists as opportunity cost. No matter what is chosen, it is always at the expense of the next best alternative which cannot then be achieved. The opportunity cost is the cost of an option in terms of the foregone alternative and is a measure of the real cost or sacrifice. The real cost does not change as a result of inflation but is relative to other costs. It is only the cost in terms of money which rises with inflation.

Feasibility studies provide an objective approach to evaluating competing proposals. The assessment of projects enables comparisons to be made between alternatives. The best option can then be adopted.

Before deciding on the best solution, it is necessary to define the critical economic objectives, namely those needs which are required to be satisfied. Only when the aims of the project are themselves decided is one in a position to find the best way of achieving them.

If the aim is to maximise returns on investments, the investor must be sure that it is not possible to spend a given sum on an alternative project with a higher return. In fact every last pound invested must return the highest possible income, otherwise it would be possible to increase revenues by investing in a different scheme. The concept of the last pound is called the *marginal unit of capital*. The return from the last unit of capital is known as the *marginal efficiency of capital* and is the figure that should be maximised, in order to maximise total returns. The reason for this

6

surprising objective is that decisions are always taken at the margin. It is always a matter of a little more or a little less. This is one of the major contributions of economic theory to management decision making. It is central to understanding the nature of the whole process of allocating resources between competing ends. It is therefore necessary to compare the extra returns obtained by spending the last block of capital on one proposal to the returns from the next best alternative. By making this comparison one can calculate how the extra return relates to the increased expenditure which is needed to achieve it. Thus, if project A costs £10 m and project B costs £8 m, the extra expenditure necessary for project A is £2 m. And, if the returns on project A are expected to be worth £3 m and project B is expected to be £2 m, the extra return is £1 m. The extra investment of £2 m therefore generates an increased return of an extra £1 m, a relatively high rate of return.

One of the central concepts used in feasibility studies is also at the heart of welfare economics and was developed by VILFREDO PARETO (1848–1923). The nineteenth-century philosophy of Utilitarianism had suggested that projects were desirable if they provided the greatest happiness of the greatest number, even when some individuals stood to lose from the change in the status quo. PARETO, on the other hand, argued that it was not possible to compare the gains and losses of different individuals. Therefore it was not possible to say that the benefits to come could offset the losses to others.

PARETO resolved this problem of comparing individuals' gains and losses by maintaining that a particular distribution of goods was inefficient if it was possible to increase the satisfaction of at least one individual without anyone else incurring a loss of satisfaction. Thus a situation was economically efficient or optimal if the only way to improve the situation for one individual would be at the expense of someone else. In that case it would not be possible to be certain that a change would be an improvement. Therefore a given status quo might be deemed efficient or PARETO optimal.

In spite of the problems highlighted by PARETO, much effort has been invested by economists in attempting to measure the costs and benefits to various individuals and groups in society, with a view to matching the gains and losses incurred by various proposals.

At this point it is necessary to introduce the reader to the *Law of diminishing marginal utility*, because a major difficulty in making assessments concerning the extra satisfaction or utility (usefulness), derived from increased benefits, is that as wealth increases, extra satisfaction does not necessarily increase in proportion. To economists, the law of diminishing

7

marginal utility applies to extra benefits accruing to individuals. Thus, assuming everything else remains constant, the extra satisfaction derived from extra units of wealth eventually declines. An increase of wealth of £1,000, for instance through tax concessions, will tend to make less difference to a wealthy individual's welfare than the same amount given to a poor person. Similarly, a loss of £1,000 to a wealthy household may only affect savings, whereas the same amount taken from less well off families will tend to result in reductions in their quality of life, as they are forced to cut their spending. It is therefore not sufficient simply to evaluate gains and losses. It is also necessary to consider their distribution between various income groups in society.

Types of feasibility study

There are as many forms of feasibility study as there are problems to solve. Different situations, different clients and different questions all require different approaches to examining the feasibility of a project. This book is largely concerned with feasibility studies in the construction industry, relating to buildings and civil engineering proposals, though broadly similar principles apply to all investment decisions. Only in matters of detail are feasibility studies in the construction field any different from those taking place in other spheres of industrial and economic activity. In the world of finance the same criteria are used in investment analysis; in industry the techniques are used in project evaluation. The major distinction to be made, however, is the quantitative one which arises when projects are so large that they have a measurable effect on third parties, that is, others in society not directly involved. In economics, these implications for others are known as *spillover* or *third party* effects. The fact of the matter is that not all the costs of a building project are borne by the client and not all the benefits are acquired by him either. The distribution of costs and benefits between losers and gainers will vary from scheme to scheme and the share of the costs and benefits which third parties pay or receive can determine a project's economic viability.

The clients of feasibility studies concerned with construction projects may be developers, local authorities, government departments or interested third parties, usually organised groups of objectors. It is clear from this list of clients that feasibility studies are often commissioned by individuals or organisations, which are subjective in that they may wish to promote a particular point of view. Often there is a pressure to present studies to support one side or the other, by strengthening a case using scientific economic arguments. In fact, feasibility studies will provide conclusions by a process of deduction from a set of assumptions. They provide a method of mustering arguments in favour and against a proposal, as well as providing decision makers with an insight into the choices open to them. Often such choices make implicit assumptions. By making these assumptions explicit, the validity of conclusions can be analysed by reference to each assumption in turn.

Before management decisions can be taken, especially major decisions concerning the siting, design and construction or adaptation of buildings, it is usually advisable to investigate the choices or options available together with the likely consequences of actions selected. Moreover, a framework is needed for all those involved, in order for them to co-operate in finding an understanding of the reasoning behind decisions. In this way all those involved or affected by a construction proposal may contribute towards influencing the final outcome. Those involved range from the client, architects, quantity surveyors, structural and service engineers, site mananger and building users to the local planning authority, politicians and interested third parties, including conservation groups and those living or working in the neighbourhood of the site of the proposal. Such a framework is supplied when feasibility studies are conducted. *for whole project*

The role of aims and objectives

Often objectives will be assumed, but it is invariably helpful for these to be made explicit in the feasibility study. As stated above, until objectives have been clearly defined, there can be no such thing as an economic solution, since what is appropriate for one situation may not be appropriate for another. However, it is reasonable to suggest that aims may include the provision of buildings for various purposes, the reduction of energy costs, the creation of a public presence or image for a company or local authority and the minimisation of building and maintenance costs. These objectives are not always compatible by any means. It is perfectly possible that a building with minimal maintenance costs might incur relatively high energy consumption; or, a building fit for a given purpose might not be possible to erect within a given budget. Often several options emerge, each capable of satisfying the stated objectives to a greater or lesser extent. Each option will have its own advantages and disadvantages and the final evaluation will rest with the client, the

9

decision maker or whoever commissioned the feasibility study in the first place.

The important point is that judgement will be based on a knowledge of the possible economic and financial implications and consequences. Certainly, it has to be said that one of the primary purposes of a feasibility study is to reject those options which are not viable; that is, those options whose costs are greater than the benefits. Most often the benefits which are taken into account are the financial ones; the profit to the developer after all other costs and taxes have been paid, or in other cases, the least cost of providing a set project at a given quality or standard, if a local authority or public sector body acts as the client.

Knowing the costs and benefits is, however, not sufficient. It is also necessary to know when they occur. Not only is it essential to understand the timing of all payments in order to plan the cash flow of the project, but also the very profitability of a given scheme will depend on the expected period of construction, date of commissioning and anticipated useful life.

Feasibility studies thus seek to establish whether or not a given proposal is worthwhile, taking the time factor into account. To do this a proposal must satisfy several objective criteria, such as net discounted present values, internal rates of return, annual equivalent value, terminal values and payback periods (or preferably, cumulative net present values), may all be used to make comparisons. These accounting criteria, which will be dealt with in chapter 3, form the core of most feasibility studies. Like any mathematical statistic, they summarise data which, in this instance, consist of the costs and benefits of each project. The calculations serve to reduce the labyrinth of variables to manageable proportions producing figures that may be easily digested by decision makers.

 Feasibility studies should also take into account any difficulties that might be anticipated, such as the effect or impact a proposal may have on a given neighbourhood. Apart from the social responsibility of individuals, there may be legal constraints on the use of a particular site. It is therefore necessary to consider the problems faced by others in the community, if only because to ignore them may lead to delays in the planning stages and increased costs for the client.

In this context there is a distinction between economic viability and financial viability. It is quite possible for a firm wishing to build a factory to see it as a financial proposition, especially when there exists a buoyant demand for the firm's product. However, although the profitability of the venture makes the factory financially viable, pollution, inconvenience and danger to the local population may render the project economically unfeasible. This would occur if it could be demonstrated that the disadvantages to those in the local community outweighed the benefits to the owners of the firm; for example, if a factor polluted a river and the number of people losing the leisure facilities offered by the river for fishing, swimming and enjoyment outweighed the value of the profits to the factory owner.

The global outcome of such decisions is not always to prevent the building of such factories but to shift their construction to another region or country where the law or the local citizenry are less well equipped to combat the threat. Moreover, it is increasingly appreciated especially since the Chernobyl disaster, that simply moving environmental hazards to another country does not necessarily avoid the risk to the global environment.

Probability and decision trees

Although this book concentrates on cost benefit analysis, it must be borne in mind that there are alternative approaches to studying feasibility. Decision theory and social decision theory may be useful methods, depending on specific circumstances and particular questions, which might be raised.

Several forms of decision aiding tools have been refined to meet these differing needs and to answer various questions. MERKHOFER identifies three main types of decision making approaches; *decision theory, social decision theory* and *cost benefit analysis*.

Decision theory is designed to help individual decision makers faced with choices which might result in a series of events or many complex outcomes. Such problems may be resolved by reference to decision trees, which provide a systematic way of considering the probabilities of various events occurring as a consequence of following particular options or decision paths. This method of evaluating decisions is based on probability theory. The two most common applications of probability theory consist of the addition rule and the multiplication rule. Probability theory assumes equal chances and random selection of events, unless otherwise stated.

The addition rule

The probability of alternatives must be added together and the sum of all probabilities must be 1. Thus, if the probability of an event occurring is 0.6, (usually written p = 0.6, or 60 per cent), then the chance of it not taking place is 0.4, (q = 0.4 or 40 per cent). The sum of p and q is 1, which means that 1 is the probability of a given event taking place and 0 the probability that it will not. Certainty therefore has a probability of 1, while impossibility has a probability value of 0.

The multiplication rule

The multiplication rule is used when an event is conditional on another event occurring first. Thus, if an event has a one in ten chance of occurring (p = 0.1), and if there is a one in two chance (c = 0.5) of a necessary precondition being satisfied, then the chance of the event actually taking place is one in twenty or 0.05, since 0.05 = 0.1 × 0.5.

A simple example will illustrate the application of the above rules. Suppose there are 50 individuals in two rooms, 10 in one room and 40 in another. If each person, regardless of which room he or she is in, buys a raffle ticket, each has a one in 50 chance of winning, (p = 0.02). The sum of the probabilities of any one individual actually winning is 1, implying that it is a certainty that one individual will win. If each person has an equal chance of drawing the winning ticket, then the probability that the winning ticket will belong to someone in the room with 10 people is a 10 in 50 chance, (or 1 in 5 or 1/5 or p = 0.2). There is clearly a 40 in 50 chance of the winning ticket belonging to someone in the other room, (q = 0.8). Again p + q = 1.

Now assume a highly deranged person armed with a gun enters the building in order to take a hostage and sees the two identical doors leading to the two rooms with 40 people in one and 10 in the other. If he decides to open one of the doors, assuming there is an equal chance of the visitor opening either door, p and q for each door are equal and both are equal to 0.5. Now the chances of an individual in the room containing 10 people finding himself being taken hostage by the intruder is 1 in 10, (p = 0.1) assuming his is the room chosen by the gunman. The probability of being chosen is therefore 0.5 × 0.1 = 0.05 or 1 in 20. For an individual in the other room containing 40 people, the probability is 1 in 40 or p = 0.025 if that room is chosen. Therefore, the chance of being the hostage for an individual in the larger group is only 0.5 × 0.025 = 0.0125 or 1 in 80. Making a decision about self preservation under these circumstances, may therefore be based on the probabilities of being taken hostage.

Decision
$\nearrow$ Door A p $=0.5\rightarrow10$ people p $=0.1\rightarrow$ hostage p $=0.05$

$\searrow$ Door B p $=0.5\rightarrow40$ people p $=0.025\rightarrow$ hostage p $=0.0125$

In other words, 10 people have a probability of 0.05 of being taken hostage and 40 people have a probability of 0.0125 of the same fate. The sum of all individuals' chances of being taken prisoner is 1; that is, there is an assumption that someone will indeed be taken as an hostage.

In making management decisions it will often be necessary to carry out an analysis by weighting the probabilities with the cost of the occurrence to find the relative value of each option. If a monetary value, such as a cost of an accident, is associated with a given event then the value of the expected event is the cost multiplied by the probability of the event occurring. The assessment of probabilities and costs is often based on informed guesswork and forms part of the assumptions of this method of arriving at a decision.

Social decision theory

The second type of decision tool identified above is based on social decision theory. Here, the decision problem arises out of the interaction of various individuals or groups attempting to make a choice, which will satisfy everyone. One method used to establish individual preferences is to survey the target population by taking a random or structured sample. Various techniques may be applied to find the intensity of approval or disapproval of different proposals by using questionnaires. Surveys may be conducted in interviews in the street, the homes of the interviewees, by phone or by post.

Whichever method is used there are many practical difficulties in applying the results uncritically. Bias may enter the figures as a result of a biased sample or interviewer influence. Again, as stated earlier, it is not possible to compare directly the loss to one individual with the gain to another. Not only are practical compromises necessary but theoretical objections, demonstrated by K J ARROW, show that any conclusions will be far from logically sound. ARROW has argued that given three individuals, each with their own set of preferences, if individual A prefers option 1 to option 2 to option 3, and if B prefers 2 to 3 to 1 and C prefers 3 to 1 to 2, there is no means of deducing a compromise solution which takes individual preferences into account. In this example, all options have equal support.

Cost benefit theory

The third type of decision tool is cost benefit theory. Cost benefit analysis is an example of a modelling device used to simplify the real world in order to focus attention on the most important and relevant issues. A model may consist of a set of equations or a set of statements or a combination of both. The model will contain inputs or independent variables and outputs or dependent variables. The purpose of a model is to describe the relationships between component parts as well as the whole model and its environment. By describing these relationships, the model may be used to predict the consequences of decisions to alter inputs. Economic models may be as large as a national economy or even global in scale or as small as individual projects and proposals. This type of approach is most useful when decisions are of a complex and technical nature.

As a simplification of the real world, the results have to be carefully interpreted before being applied. Again, this tool is no device for the scientific or logical purist. Judgement is required at every step in the assessment of costs and benefits, especially when these do not involve goods and services bought and sold in markets. However, it should be remembered that even where goods are bought and sold, their prices are not always easy to determine in advance and, when they are, these prices may not reflect the value of the goods to society. Variations in property valuations and tender prices are great, and predicting them depends on an interpretation of current market conditions and an assessment of expectations.

Although described separately above, all three types of decision making approach may be used in combination in any feasibility study. Techniques developed in one area may usefully be applied in the context of any of the three approaches. This book concentrates mainly on cost benefit theory and its derivative, cost benefit analysis. There are two reasons for this emphasis. *Firstly*, cost benefit analysis is the most useful approach to apply to building proposals, with complex interactions with the site, local population and planning authorities as well as the environment. *Secondly*, it is the method largely adopted by professionals in the field; the economists, accountants, bankers, quantity surveyors, developers and, increasingly, those in government departments.

It is not possible to provide a pro forma feasibility study into which data for each proposal might be inserted to produce definitive answers and take decisions. Aspects of all the above approaches might be used in any one feasibility report. Each study should be tailored to the needs and circumstances in operation at the time. A model feasibility study would result in many cases in irrelevant information being collected and inappropriate measures being used. The results of any feasibility study need to be carefully interpreted and indeed the study should only be seen as part of the process of decision making and design. Every method used to study and predict feasibility has its weaknesses and limitations and these should be recognised, articulated and taken into account in making an assessment of the results. Often, a feasibility study is little more than a systematic presentation of the arguments, constructed in such a way that decision makers may view all the relevant implications of their decisions.

Summary

Feasibility studies represent a decision making approach with a long history. Though the techniques still require refinement they offer a systematic approach to establishing the likely outcome of decisions and the costs involved. Though these predictions about the future are by no means certain, their usefulness lies in the hope that the results may be nearer to expectations if they are based on an objective assessment of the costs and benefits of a scheme, rather than if decisions are based purely on intuition. If the results are more often correct than other methods of prediction, then the exercise may be said to be worthwhile undertaking.

Moreover, using cost benefit analysis, it is possible to relate detailed analyses of building costs to complex notional costs which might only arise in the far distant future. With the increasing awareness of environmental and ecological problems which are accumulating in the world at an alarming rate, it is likely that building projects with expected useful lives of 50 to 100 years must begin to anticipate some of these future implications, especially those relating to energy use and pollution as well as the consumption of diminishing raw material resources.

References

[1] ROGERS, AK, *A Student's History of Philosophy*, 3rd edition, Macmillan 1929 and 1935 p 439.
[2] ibid p 435.
[3] ibid p 440.
[4] HEARDER, H, *Europe In The Nineteenth Century 1830/1880*, Longman 1966 p 339.
[5] PLAMENATZ J, *Man and Society*, Vol 2, Longman 1963 p 79.
[6] MERKHOFER, MW, *Decision Science and Social Risk Management*, Reidel 1987 p 60.

two

The layout of feasibility studies

Introduction

Why commission or write a feasibility study in the first place? One of the functions of a feasibility study is to establish, in advance of any major expense and commitment, the capital and running costs of a building proposal and its likely revenues and hence profitability. There is no one format for conducting a feasibility study. The structure and the information included in a study will depend on the questions the client wishes to have answered and whether the building is required for the client for sale on completion or for owner occupation. Questions may include those concerning environmental impact, effects on unemployment and profitability of the scheme. It must be conceded, however, that the benefits or savings in running costs are not always used in marketing a building. Savings in the cost of operating a building are not necessarily passed on to the buyers, who in any case do not always take future building operating costs and maintenance fully into account. These may be seen as unavoidable expenses which are often dwarfed by other running costs such as staff salaries.

The decision maker may be in a different department from the managers who will eventually control the building, in which case the running costs are dealt with by a separate department. Furthermore, the tax system in the UK has tended to favour buildings with low initial and high annual running costs. Whilst capital costs are not deductible against corporation tax, maintenance costs are.

Nevertheless, it is likely that if reduced running costs are communicated to possible tenants or buyers, the selling price of the property may be enhanced to share the benefits between developer and owner occupier. Moreover, it is likely that a building which is cheaper to operate than another will also be easier to re-sell at the end of its planned period of use or earlier.

The feasibility study will, or ought to, point out which factors are critical to the success of a proposal; for instance, the timing of the project, interest rates, the rate of inflation, other developments taking place or planned in the vicinity of the site, the local infrastructure and third party objections. The feasibility study should also show how a project will meet the financial, economic and aesthetic demands made of it.

Feasibility studies may be used for a variety of purposes. They will enable the original brief to be examined in more detail, prompting discussions of objectives, costs and implications of the proposal. This dialogue between the client and his professional advisers can be focused on the feasibility study in order to plan a project with consistency. It will highlight any contractions or conflicting objectives stated in the original brief. These discussions will help to develop the proposal to meet the needs of the client, the building users, the local authority and any other groups affected by a given project.

A feasibility study can be used in approaches to financial institutions since the information concerning the viability of a project, its costs, timing and rates of return will all be of interet to banking organisations. Clearly, the project must be profitable and the feasibility study should demonstrate that the funds used to finance the project will be returned to the lender by the end of the loan period.

Another function of a feasibility study is to examine systematically a shortlisted set of options. By being systematic, the feasibility study minimises the risk that important factors may be omitted from the assessment and comparison of various alternatives. Although judgement must be exercised with regard to the valuations of all costs, the methodology applied to each scheme is to a certain extent objective in the sense that the conclusions are deduced logically from the set of assumptions fed in to the equations of the model. The validity of the conclusions therefore depends on the validity of the assumptions and these then become the focus of attention for the discussions which take place at this stage.

As part of a feasibility study is necessarily involved with the assessment of costs in advance of construction, and revenues in advance of sales or letting, it provides one of the first indicators of the budget needed for the project to be viable. It demonstrates the maximum costs and minimum revenues necessary to justify the project financially.

These figures can be analysed in terms of the building as a whole. To find the total cost per square metre, the total cost is divided by the *gross floor area* (GFA). Similarly, the cost per square metre of functional parts of a building, such as an auditorium, shop units, restaurants and circulation areas within a scheme, may be estimated using cost per square metre. Costs may also be stated in terms of functional units, such as cost per employee position or cost per bed. However, yardsticks oversimplify requirements and take insufficient account of actual costs. Cost per pupil was used by the Ministry of Education as a cost yardstick to relate costs to the basic accommodation being provided rather than the overall cost of the building, but cost per pupil is higher the smaller the school, assuming similar standards.

Using yardsticks and applying them to various buildings on different sites it was thought that a degree of consistency could be found in the costs not only of the building as a whole but also the building's elements such as its frame, external walls and mechanical services. To some extent, this consistency was the result of a self-fulfilling prophecy, since yardsticks dictate standards instead of the standards determining the costs. Satisfying the requirements set by the yardsticks themselves becomes the major objective. Far from achieving similar standards, yardsticks cause unwanted variations.

As recently as the 1970s, yardsticks for local authority housing were geared largely to the cost per bed space allowance. This resulted in local authorities designing in order to take maximum advantage of the allowances, with the result that many three and four bedroom houses were built rather than smaller starter homes for which there was a greater demand.

The variation in elemental costs varies greatly from one building to the next depending on the shape, method of construction and specification of the building. Maintaining the same cost percentages of one building may lead to a repetition of the faults arising in the first building. Differences in the quality, location and accessibility of a site can also distort figures for one building when compared to another. Regional variations and variations within regions will affect labour and material costs as pressure of work in one area may not necessarily apply in another. As SMITH points out, 'Contractors' prices are extremely sensitive ... with the result that price levels in Yorkshire and Humberside, for example, may be summarised as being 12 per cent below Outer London; however, within the region, Sheffield tends to 17 per cent below, while Bradford averages 10 per cent below'.[1] These relative figures are constantly changing to reflect the changing economic climate in each locality.

Nevertheless, elemental cost breakdowns show the allocation of resources between different parts of a building and these allocations may be compared to the range of costs for elements in similar buildings. Hence, cost planning exercises involve an elemental cost breakdown to indicate the similarity to the norm for a given building type. In this way the feasibility study is the first step in the process of controlling costs not only during the construction phase but also throughout the life of a project.

The study can be used as a basis for monitoring any project with an extended life such as a building. This is not to imply that the original feasibility study will always be used. In the course of developing a project and later during the construction phase several revisions to the first set of figures will be necessary as changes are made and unexpected difficulties or unanticipated delays occur. The monitoring of a project must therefore take into account any drift from the original proposal. However, each revision can be based on the current set of figures in order to decide whether or not a particular change will improve project or detract from the objectives.

In this way, the success or failure of the building can be measured. Successful practice can then be repeated while unsuccessful aspects can be modified and avoided in future schemes. It enables each scheme to become part of the learning experience of all those involved in managing major projects, which would benefit not only the building users and the clients but would lead to improved professional practice.

During the life of the building the feasibility study may be used to set targets for the future managers of the building, provided that the information and figures presented in the study can be updated to reflect changes in, for instance, values and prices as well as volumes of activity, numbers of people affected and quantity of sales. This process of target setting must of necessity be very flexible to take into account the changing and unpredicted requirements made of the building. Nevertheless, if a building is a machine for living and working in, then the feasibility study can be used to form the set of instructions, or at least the basis for advice as to its best use and mode of operation.

In this sense the feasibility study can be used to communicate between those who initiate a building project and those who eventually take over the job of running it. The documents of the feasibility study will enable the building's ultimate managers to gain some understanding of the original intentions of the design. This, in turn, will assist the managers of the building to run the organisation more efficiently than they otherwise would have been able to.

From the earliest stage of a project there is a need for those involved in the design and building team to communicate ideas between each other. The feasibility study enables this communication to take place. The study then remains as a point of reference for all future discussions until the project is completed. The earlier that various consultants can be brought into discussions, the faster the project can ultimately be completed. Problems at the planning stage from interested third parties to building regulations and at every stage of the construction process should be anticipated to avoid unnecessary delays and hence, reduce costs of the building. Early communication can reduce the number of designs, which have to be rejected through insufficient information in the brief. Schemes, which are sub-optimal from one point of view or another can be compared to find a compromise solution. It is not necessary for the best solution to be optimal in all its aspects. Indeed, it is likely that in order to achieve overall efficiency in the design solution, some if not all, elements will be used at below their optimum level. Clearly a device to take all conflicting interests into account is needed and the feasibility study provides one method for dealing with this problem. It is the first step in efficient project management.

Feasibility studies can be used to market projects by enabling the client to deliver presentations and answer questions with consistency. For this reason, feasibility studies are also useful devices, from the developer's point of view, for dealing with public relations. There is no reason, however, why feasibility studies cannot be used by interested third parties to object to schemes either by discussing their objections with the developer before planning permission is sought (which is unusual), or by drawing up their own feasibility study.

It is possible to place costs and benefits in various categories, depending on when they arise and whether or not actual payments are made. Thus, costs and benefits may be tangible or intangible. They are tangible if actual payments are made, because invoices are raised against the transaction and there is a legal obligation to make a payment. There is, however, a second type of tangible cost. A cost is a tangible cost if it could be charged to a project *as if* an actual price had been paid. For example, if a developer already owns a site, the site has a value, namely the opportunity cost of selling the site on to another user. The cost of the site is a tangible cost, since the developer has foregone the income from the sale.

Intangible costs and benefits are those which do not place a legal obligation on the developer to pay or for which the developer receives no recompense. Examples of intangible costs would be the loss of trade to third parties, pollution and inconvenience caused by a development to those living in its vicinity. Intangible benefits might include the improvement to an area raising its appeal for those living and working there, shorter journey times and increased safety.

Costs which are incurred at the construction and pre-construction stages are called *initial costs*. They are non-recurring costs, which only arise in the first year or two of a project. Initial tangible costs include the cost of the site, stamp duty, construction costs, architects' and other professionals' fees and local authority costs for obtaining planning permission. Initial intangible costs include the noise, dust and disruption to others, including their loss of business caused during the construction phase. Other costs which are incurred throughout the expected useful life of the building are called *annual costs* and these include payments for maintenance, services and staffing.

Similarly, benefits may be categorised according to the period in which they occur. Initial benefits are usually trivial compared to the size of the project since the building only begins to generate benefits as parts of the building are commissioned. However, certain retailers in the neighbourhood of a site might benefit from increased trade from the site workers during the construction phase.

It is often argued that building projects create employment during initial period. In fact, while it is true that the work may be a benefit to the employees and labourers, if the value of these benefits are calculated they would exactly cancel the cost of labour element in the construction cost. This would minimise the costs artificially, since the labour cost represents the value of the use of a resource on one project rather than another. However, in areas of high unemployment, building work may be seen as one of the benefits of a scheme. This is more of a political than economic argument. As such it may well form part of the argument in favour of a particular scheme, without the figures being included in the calculations concerning the viability of the project. In fact, unless the object of the scheme is simply to create employment, it is not an economic benefit of the scheme. In this context, an economic benefit may be defined as a gain resulting from the completed construction. In certain cost benefit studies employment during the construction phase is included if the model is defined to include social benefits. If unemployment is high, what economists call, 'the opportunity cost' of giving work to the unemployed will be zero, since the opportunity cost of employing someone in those circumstances does not involve a loss to society.

Suggested form of feasibility study

As feasibility studies are often read by people with little time to spare, it is important that the document should provide all the most relevant information in a pertinent and easily digestible form. Although it is desirable that the document should be brief, feasibility studies may vary in length from a few pages to several volumes containing many hundreds of thousands of words. Nevertheless, it might be worthwhile to suggest a possible format for the presentation of a typical cost benefit analysis. This is not a suggestion for a pro forma document to be applied in every situation.

According to HEUSTON: 'The basic elements of cost effectiveness analysis or cost benefit analysis have been described in many ways ... the broad categories of elements usually mentioned, include the following:

The Objective (or objectives)
The Alternatives
The Costs
A Model
A Criterion.'[2]

The model involves a description of the project over time in verbal and mathematical terms, showing the size of the project and when the costs and benefits are expected to arise. The criterion forms the basis of the decision, according to which factors are seen as critical in the eyes of the decision makers. Thus the criterion may be the rate of return, the net present value or the measure of pollution or the maximum number of people served.

The introduction to a feasibility study

The first section should be a brief introduction. This should state the aims of the building in terms of the critical factors which will influence the decision outcome. Critical factors are those aspects of the building to which the building must conform. They may include for instance, measurable variables such as area per workspace or air purity in controlled environments or building height or even not obstructing a view. Indeed non-measurable aesthetic considerations, such as the destruction of the scenic landscape, can also be taken into account. As a restatement of the aims, the introduction is direction related to the original brief.

Summary and recommendations section of a feasibility study

The summary and recommendations should state the internal rates of return of the various proposals, the net present values, annual equivalence and other relevant financial figures, such as the capital outlays involved in each option. The summary of these figures should lead to a recommendation for one of the schemes, which the writer will have found to be the one which best satisfies the objectives set in the introduction, according to the criteria of the critical factors.

The proposal statement

In this part of the report the favoured option may be discussed in more detail, in terms of costs and benefits overall, showing the wider aims of the option chosen and placing it in a social context.

Alternatives analysed and compared

The alternatives need to be discussed insofar as decisions may be taken which are different from the recommendation. It is far better to state the alternatives in full to a client than simply offering one proposal on a take it or leave it basis, just as a shoe sales person would be more likely to succeed if customers are offered a choice. Requiring clients to choose between options is a preferable marketing strategy than presenting just one scheme with the risk that it may be rejected. Moreover, it is only by making the client aware of the alternatives that he will be aware of the real cost of a particular option. The client will see what he is giving up in order to have the option of his choice. Often a combination of options or parts of alternative schemes may after further research and development, form a new solution, especially where aspects of two designs may be combined for aesthetic purposes.

Planning section in the feasibility study

As buildings are never erected in an urban or rural vacuum, it is necessary to view the proposal in a planning context, taking planning considerations into account. Again, a delay at the planning stage might render projects non-viable. Planning law is ever changing and it is important to inform clients of the procedures and limitations or restrictions, which might be imposed. Proposals must take into account easements or rights of way, light for adjoining properties, building height and materials used, as well as preservation orders. Other restrictions concern density and activities in the proposed buildings, whether industrial, commercial or residential. The proposals must comply with structure and local plans to avoid delays in gaining planning permission. Various governmental authorities should be contacted. Apart from planning permission, the local authority will also be responsible for enforcing the Building Regulations to ensure the construction of a building meets the minimum legal requirements. The local highway authority may also impose constraints on the lines of proposed buildings.

Costing details in appendix of feasibility study

In this appendix, the elemental cost breakdown will show the distribution of the total cost of construction, cost of site and other professional costs which will have been used to calculate the project's viability. The viability of any project will depend on the assumed values of costs and benefits in the analysis. It is important to state these figures in case any are not acceptable to the client.

It is quite possible to include a developer's set of accounts as well as a broader cost benefit analysis. What is presented will largely depend on the type of client and his needs.

Generally the main items of a financial analysis consists of the following checklist and these would be estimated for each option, unless the item applies equally to all, in which case it may be ignored for the purpose of decision making. For instance, if staffing levels are identical for different options, then staffing costs may be ignored.

Checklist of major cost categories

INITIAL COSTS, arising at the commencement of a buildings existence

Cost of site
    Purchase price
    Stamp duty
    Legal fees
    Finance costs

Cost of construction
    Cost per sq m
    Architect's fees
    Quantity Surveyor's fees
    Engineer's fees
    Finance costs
    Building regulations

Cost of letting
    Estate agent's fees
    Advertising/marketing costs

Cost of furnishing and fitting, (where appropriate)

ANNUAL REVENUES AND COSTS, arising after completion

Annual revenues
    Expected annual rental income
    Expected annual sales income

Annual costs
    Services
    Maintenance
    Local property taxes
    Staffing
    Insurance

References

[1] SMITH, R, 'Cost Information Sources', *Architects' Journal*, 17 August 1983 p 51.
[2] HEUSTON, MC, 'Cost Benefit Analysis at the SHAPE Technical Cebtre', in KENDALL, MG, ed, *Cost Benefit Analysis*, English Universities Press 1971 p 141.

three

Introduction to discounting techniques

Introduction

As mentioned in chapters 1 and 2, various criteria may be used to evaluate proposals. This chapter examines these procedures to see which are the most appropriate in different circumstances.

Since decisions are taken at the beginning of a project, the values of costs and benefits which arise in the future need to be brought to a comparable point in time. This is usually calculated using discounting techniques to find their equivalent values at the initial period of the project. In some instances, it is desirable to monitor projects throughout their anticipated life and this may be achieved by calculating either the terminal value or the annual equivalence. The terminal value provides a valuation of the project net of costs on disposal of the assets at some point in the future.

Alternatively, the project may be monitored annually by reference only to the cost of operating the scheme, taking all costs including the costs of finance and repayment of loans into account. The annual equivalence criterion may be used to assume that the benefits are independent of costs and that the client's main concern is to achieve a given purpose at minimum annual cost. This method, known as cost effectiveness may also be applied to the other financial criteria, where the benefits of each option are deemed to be so similar that only cost comparisons are required.

Benefit cost ratios are also often used to compare proposals of differing size. The benefit cost ratio relates the size of benefits to the cost of obtaining them. Other criteria include incremental analysis, which examines the increase in gains as a result of an investment compared to the increase in costs necessary to bring about the extra benefits. Only if the value of the extra benefits is greater than the extra cost and the rate of return greater than the rate of interest is the proposal worth considering. The capital cost of various projects has to be seen in terms of the amounts of finance available to fund projects. Therefore, regardless of the advantages of various schemes, if the capital expenditure were beyond the limits or borrowing capacity of the developer then the scheme would not be considered feasible. However, this constraint on the budget may be more flexible in practice than first appears, since financially viable projects will often receive financial backing from outside banking institutions, by virtue of their financial viability. These then are the major criteria used in cost benefit analysis.

Cost benefit analysis

Cost benefit analysis encompasses the whole range of costs and benefits which arise. It takes into account that costs may be shared with those not directly involved in the construction of the project. At the same time it recognises that many individuals often benefit from projects to which they themselves have made no direct contribution. The major difficulty, however, is taking into account the actual distribution of these costs and benefits. A weakness of cost benefit analysis is the need to aggregate the costs and benefits to establish which total is the greater and by how much. This approach may disregard the distribution of costs and benefits though the spread of gains and losses can be built in to the model by weighting the figures used. Thus, extra weights may be given to groups which the decision makers perceive to merit extra attention in the study.

Nevertheless, cost benefit studies have their uses in so far as they bring to light many assumptions which will be implicit in any scheme. Moreover, the variables are all combined in one systematic framework which enables sensitivity analysis to be conducted to establish the degree of risk, the minimum values that might be assumed before projects cease to be viable and using Monte Carlo techniques, the most likely outcome if the project were to go ahead. Indeed, a risk profile can be found showing the probability of various outcomes against their expected net present values.

Discounting techniques

At the core of a feasibility study is the mathematical or accounting model used to combine the raw data or financial information which will have been collected from various sources, such as quantity surveyors, manufacturers, suppliers and widely available architects' and builders' price books.

This financial modelling technique involves discounting money in the future to give it a present value. Money at some point in the future is not worth as much as money today. The longer the wait for payment the less the present value of the future amount. This time dimension of money would exist even in a world without interest rates or inflation. Known as the *rate of time preference* (TPR), it will vary from one individual to the next depending on the individual's or company's circumstances, requirements, age and tastes. An average figure for a whole economy is known as the *social rate of time preference*. The difference in value between the same amount of money in two periods of time may be calculated using a discount rate. A discount rate is equivalent to a compound rate of interest but instead of calculating a future value from a present amount of money, the discount rate is used in the reverse direction to equate the future figure with a present value. Thus, assuming a TPR of 10 per cent, £100 in one year's time is worth only £90.90 today. The discount rate less the rate of inflation is the net discount rate, which takes into account the erosion over time of the purchasing power of an investment.

As far as buildings are concerned, because they are constructed in one period and remain in existence for many decades, all expected benefits accruing to owners in years to come must be discounted before they can be added to benefits accruing in the near future. Similarly, anticipated costs incurred in the figure also have to be discounted. All values have to be discounted to a common period before final aggregation can be carried out. Usually the period chosen is the current, because decisions have to be taken in the present. However, any period can be used, by simply compounding figures which arise in earlier periods to the selected year and discounting the later years back to the same period. The use of the word 'discount' in this context is no different from the familiar use when purchasing an item at a discount, which implies a reduction from the face value.

To compound a certain amount of money to the future, the basic formula is:

$$\text{Present value} \times (1+r)^i = \text{Future value}$$

and to discount a known future sum back to the present, the formula becomes:

$$\text{Present value} = \frac{1}{(1+r)^i} \times \text{Future value}$$

In the formulae, r is the discount rate expressed as a fraction and i represents the number of years hence. Thus the present value of £1,000 in two years at a discount rate of 10 per cent pa is;

$$\text{Present value} = \frac{1}{(1+0.1)^2} \times \pounds 1{,}000$$

$$= \frac{1}{1.1^2} \times \pounds 1{,}000$$

$$= \frac{1}{1.21} \times \pounds 1{,}000$$

$$= 0.826446 \times \pounds 1{,}000$$
$$= \pounds 826.45$$

Although calculating the discount factor is straightforward, it is laborious to find the many factors needed for each year and then discount these figures at the rate selected. Discount factor tables based on the above formula are widely available and simple to use. Indeed, many computer spreadsheet programs include discounting so that the actual computation of present values can be rapid. Computerisation of discounting techniques facilitates carrying out sensitivity analyses, making it possible to alter the value of variables at will or when new information becomes available. A sensitivity analysis simply shows what the consequences would be if, for instance, wage inflation were to be 8 or10 per cent, if sales were to rise at 10 or 15 per cent per annum or if the building were to be delayed by six months or a year.

If only tangible costs and benefits are calculated, discounting techniques can be applied to establish the *net present value* (NPV). The NPV is the current value of a proposal after costs have been deducted from revenues. The NPV is a measure of the increase in the value of a company's assets. The higher the discount rate the lower the net present value (just as the higher the discount on a washing machine, the lower its price). The choice of discount rate depends on various factors including the firm's cost of borrowing and the rate of inflation. To this rate, which would have to be paid to the lender, such as a bank, must be added a risk loading associated with a given proposal and a buffer to enable interest rates to rise without jeopardising the project. Discounting techniques are then applied to all benefits and all costs. Alternatively, the discount rate used may be equal to the rate of return of an alternative investment, which the client would otherwise be able to undertake.

If the discounted benefits are greater than the discounted costs then the proposal will have a positive NPV. This implies that at the given rate of discount, there will be an appreciation in the value of the capital, equivalent to that difference. In other words, if an investment of

£1,000,000 generates a net present value of £150,000, then the value of the investment costing £1,000,000 is £1,150,000 immediately and by virtue of the decision taken to go ahead with the proposal. If the net present value were to come out negatively, then the assets of the investor will be depleted by the same amount.

Yield and internal rate of return

A yield is a percentage rate of return on an investment. The simplest method of estimating the yield is to take the net revenue from the first normal year of operation and calculate it as a percentage of the capital investment. Thus, if a building cost £10 m to construct and the annual rent is expected to be £1 per annum, the yield is taken as:

$$\frac{£1}{£10} \times 100 = 10\%$$

However, this measure is only a rough and ready approximation. It assumes, for instance, that the returns after all costs have been met will always be £1 per annum. A more flexible calculation of yield, taking into account different future flows of money is the *internal rate of return* (IRR).

The internal rate of return is a discount rate. It is in fact the special case or rate which occurs when the discounted costs and benefits throughout the expected life of the building are equal. The internal rate of return is like an interest rate generated by a project on the amount invested in it. In a sense the internal rate of return of money deposited in a bank at 5 per cent interest per annum is 5 per cent. If the IRR of a project is found to be, say 14 per cent, then if the developer were required to pay interest at 14 per cent, there would be sufficient funds to service the loan but no other surplus or profit.

To calculate the internal rate of return of a project, the question to be answered is, what discount rate if applied to the costs and benefits will exactly equate them? It is possible to plot net present values against various discount rates. When the rate is high, as pointed out above, the net present value will be low or even negative. When a rate of discount produces a net present value equal to zero, there would be neither a gain or loss in the value of the capital assets of the organisation, if the cost of borrowing were equal to that discount rate. At lower rates of interest, there would be a profit; at higher rates, a loss.

It is common for the NPV and IRR criteria to favour different options.

This apparent contradiction would occur if the NPV of one option were higher than another option with a higher IRR. This highlights the need to interpret the results with care and to avoid making decisions on the basis of only one criterion. A management decision should rest on a combination of an understanding of the economic criteria and the particular circumstances.

There are two ways of dealing with seemingly contradictory results. The first simply gives NPV precedence over the IRR and the second adopts incremental analysis.

The logic of the first argument giving NPV precedence over IRR is as follows. Assume two proposals X and Y are put forward, as shown in table 3.1. The first, X, requires an investment of £100 and offers a profit £100 within a given period of time (a rate of return of 100 per cent). The second proposition, Y, calls for an investment of £1,000 and promises to return a profit of £500 in the same period as the first proposal (in this instance, a rate of return of only 50 per cent). Given a choice between profits of £100 for option X and £500 for option Y, the rational decision maker would choose Y, though the rate of return is half that of X, assuming the decision maker had £1,000 to invest in the first place and both proposals carried equal risk. The option with the higher rate of return only generates £100, while the lower rate of return produces a much larger surplus, which therefore enables the decision maker to go on to purchase more goods and services than would be available to him if the first choice had been taken.

Table 3.1   *Comparison of two options*

	Capital required £	Profit £	Rate of return £
Option X	100	100	100
Option Y	1,000	500	50
Y − X	900	400	44

The logic of incremental analysis is based on a comparison of the value of the extra gain and the extra costs incurred? For instance, one might wish to purchase a new car from a garage. The basic model, without any 'extras' costs £6,000. The next model up in the range costs £6,400. For the extra £400 the customer receives a radio and extra trim on the doors. In effect, the customer has to decide whether to pay £400 for a radio and the trim. Of course, the final decision is subjective but the decision has been simplified by considering only the extra benefits and extra costs.

Indeed the next stage of the decision making process may be to consider the cost of buying and installing an identical car radio from an alternative supplier. Assume that the cost of doing this is £250. The decision has now been reduced to the opportunity cost of £400 for the integrated radio and trim or £250 for the separate radio, which would leave £150 over. Assuming a radio is essential for the car, the cost of the trim is £150 to the purchaser. One factor which often enters such decisions is the inconvenience factor and often consumers will buy a more expensive product combination to avoid difficulties and time wasting. At any rate, incremental analysis is basically an application of the same principles used by many buyers in everyday life.

In the financial example above, the extra profits of £400 are produced by increasing investment by £900, producing a rate of return of 44 per cent. This rate of return on the last £900 has to be compared to the cost of borrowing and its opportunity cost and, provided it is above them, the extra investment can be justified.

An examination of discounted cash flow tables below will help to demonstrate the use of the NPV and the IRR. The value of the NPV in this example uses a target rate of return of 15 per cent. This target figure may be based on the current rate of interest charged to borrowers plus a 'buffer' to allow for the risk of increases in the rate. Assume a brief for an office development, required by the client for owner occupation for at least 13 years and a maximum budget of £8 m, all payments to be made at the beginning of each year and all funding to be externally financed. After discussions with the client, two solutions emerge as possibilities. The cash flow of the first option, option A, is shown in table 3.2. For simplicity, all cash flows in this example ignore inflation.

Option A costs £8 m and because of the use of superior materials requires no major refurbishment for 20 years. The value of the building on disposal or sale in real terms at the beginning of the fifteenth year of the project is assumed to be twice the size of the original investment at £16 m. The expected annual net income is calculated to be £1.6 m. The IRR is 21.23 per cent and the NPV is £3.19 m.

A second, far cheaper option, option B, shown in table 3.3 is found to have an IRR of 27.65 per cent but an NPV of only £2.5 m. Option B's figures are based on a capital investment of £3 m, an expected disposal value of £8 m and annual net revenues of £0.8 m, except in the tenth year of the building when a major refurbishment is planned, reducing net income in that year to £0.4 m. If the NPV is used to select the option, then option A's £3.19 m will be preferred to option B's £2.5 m. Nevertheless, some managers argue that as the IRR of option B is greater than

Table 3.2

	Option A				Discount rates	
Year	*Cost*	*Benefit*	*Net Ben.*	*5%*	*10%*	*15%*
1	8	0	−8	−8.0	−8.0	−8.0
2	0.3	1.9	1.6	1.523810	1.454545	1.391304
3	0.3	1.9	1.6	1.451247	1.322314	1.209830
4	0.3	1.9	1.6	1.382140	1.202104	1.052026
5	0.3	1.9	1.6	1.316324	1.092822	0.914805
6	0.3	1.9	1.6	1.253642	0.993474	0.795483
7	0.3	1.9	1.6	1.193945	0.903158	0.691724
8	0.3	1.9	1.6	1.137090	0.821053	0.601499
9	0.3	1.9	1.6	1.082943	0.746411	0.523043
10	0.3	1.9	1.6	1.031374	0.678556	0.454820
11	0.3	1.9	1.6	0.982261	0.616869	0.395496
12	0.3	1.9	1.6	0.935486	0.560790	0.343909
13	0.3	1.9	1.6	0.890939	0.509809	0.299051
14	0.3	1.9	1.6	0.848514	0.463463	0.260045
15		16	16	8.081087	4.213300	2.261259
Net Discounted Present Value				15.11080	7.578670	3.194294
The Internal Rate of Return				21.23		

Table 3.3

	Option B				Discount rates	
Year	*Cost*	*Benefit*	*Net Ben.*	*5%*	*10%*	*15%*
1	3	0	−3	−3.0	−3.0	−3.0
2	0.3	1.1	0.8	0.761905	0.727273	0.695652
3	0.3	1.1	0.8	0.725624	0.661157	0.604915
4	0.3	1.1	0.8	0.691070	0.601052	0.526013
5	0.3	1.1	0.8	0.658162	0.546411	0.457403
6	0.3	1.1	0.8	0.626821	0.496737	0.397741
7	0.3	1.1	0.8	0.596972	0.451579	0.345862
8	0.3	1.1	0.8	0.568545	0.410527	0.300750
9	0.3	1.1	0.8	0.541472	0.373206	0.261521
10	0.3	1.1	0.8	0.515687	0.339278	0.227410
11	0.5	0.9	0.4	0.245565	0.154217	0.098874
12	0.3	1.1	0.8	0.467743	0.280395	0.171955
13	0.3	1.1	0.8	0.445470	0.254905	0.149525
14	0.3	1.1	0.8	0.424257	0.231732	0.130022
15		8	8	4.040544	2.10665	1.130629
Net Discounted Present Value				8.309837	4.635118	2.498273
The Internal Rate of Return				27.65		

option A's, option B shows an ability to pay a higher rate of interest, and in case interest rates rise, the risk associated with option B would be less than option A. The IRR therefore shows the option with the lower financial risk. The argument between NPV and IRR is between profit maximisation and risk minimisation.

Table 3.4

	Option A – Option B				*Discount rates*	
Year	*Opt. A*	*Opt. B*	*A – B*	*5%*	*10%*	*15%*
1	−8	−3	−5	−5.0	−5.0	−5.0
2	1.6	0.8	0.8	0.761905	0.727273	0.695652
3	1.6	0.8	0.8	0.725624	0.661157	0.604915
4	1.6	0.8	0.8	0.691070	0.601052	0.526013
5	1.6	0.8	0.8	0.658162	0.546411	0.457403
6	1.6	0.8	0.8	0.626821	0.496737	0.397741
7	1.6	0.8	0.8	0.596972	0.451579	0.345862
8	1.6	0.8	0.8	0.568545	0.410526	0.300750
9	1.6	0.8	0.8	0.541471	0.373206	0.261521
10	1.6	0.8	0.8	0.515687	0.339278	0.227410
11	1.6	0.4	1.2	0.736696	0.462652	0.296622
12	1.6	0.8	0.8	0.467743	0.280395	0.171955
13	1.6	0.8	0.8	0.445467	0.254904	0.149526
14	1.6	0.8	0.8	0.424257	0.231731	0.130022
15	16	8	8	4.040545	2.106650	1.130629
Net Discounted Present Value				6.800967	2.943552	0.6960207
The Internal Rate of Return				17.23		

Table 3.4 illustrates the extra returns on the extra capital invested if the £8 m project is chosen instead of the option costing £3 m. In return for the extra £5 m capital outlay, the extra expected revenue would be £0.8 m per annum apart from the tenth year when the extra income would be £1.2 m. The extra value on disposal would be £8 m. Calculating the returns on the extra investment yields an IRR of 17.23 per cent and an NPV of £0.7 m. Clearly, as long as interest rates remain below 17 per cent, it will be financially worthwhile borrowing the extra £5 m. If a target rate of return of 15 per cent is used to accept or reject projects then option A would be acceptable, since the NPV is still positive at that rate.

However, if the client had an alternative possibility, say, developing a shopping centre, in which he could invest the last £5 m, then a comparison must be made to find the best use for the money. Table 3.5 illustrates option C for a different site than the one chosen for the office scheme.

Table 3.5

		Option C			Discount rates	
Year	*Cost*	*Benefit*	*Net Ben.*	*5%*	*10%*	*15%*
1	4	0	−4	−4.0	−4.0	−4.0
2	0.3	1.5	1.2	1.142857	1.090909	1.043478
3	0.3	1.5	1.2	1.088435	0.991735	0.907372
4	0.3	1.5	1.2	1.036605	0.901577	0.789019
5	0.3	1.5	1.2	0.987243	0.819616	0.686103
6	0.3	1.5	1.2	0.940231	0.745105	0.596612
7	0.3	1.5	1.2	0.895458	0.677368	0.518793
8	0.3	1.5	1.2	0.852817	0.615789	0.451124
9	0.3	1.5	1.2	0.812207	0.559809	0.392282
10	0.3	1.5	1.2	0.773530	0.508917	0.341115
11	0.5	1.2	0.7	0.429749	0.269880	0.173029
12	0.3	1.5	1.2	0.701615	0.420592	0.257932
13	0.3	1.5	1.2	0.668205	0.382357	0.224288
14	0.3	1.5	1.2	0.636386	0.347597	0.195033
15		12	12	6.060815	3.159975	1.695944
Net Discounted Present Value				13.02615	7.491231	4.272128
The Internal Rate of Return				30.97		

Option C involves an investment of £4 m, with an expected annual net income of £1.2 m, except in the tenth year when repairs and refurbishment reduce the net revenues to £0.7 m. The disposal value of this scheme is expected to be £12 m. The NPV of option C is over £4.27 m, compared to less than £1 m in return for spending the extra £5 m on option A rather than option B. The choice now lies between adopting option B costing £8 m or adopting both option A costing £3 m together with option C costing £4 m. The financial recommendation would be to opt for projects B and C, costing £7 m in total but increasing the asset value of the firm by £20 m. Option A would only have increased asset values by £16 m.

Costs in use

An alternative but closely related method of evaluating projects is by calculating annual equivalence. This broadly speaking means finding out how much a project would cost to run and finance on an annual basis. This method is particularly appropriate when the projects being compared are of widely differing duration, as much as 60 years for office developments or 30 years for industrial buildings.

Costs have to be split between those needed for the day-to-day running and maintenance of a building and the repayment of funds required to construct the building in the first place. An annual amount of money must be set aside each year to allow for the replacement of the building at the end of its life, otherwise, the firm, say an owner occupier, will have simply used up its capital and be left with no funds at the end of the planned period. This annual sum is called *the sinking fund*, and each year's allocation of money for the sinking fund will itself earn interest until the fund is required. Clearly the longer the period of time, the easier it is to repay any loans as the principal can be divided into smaller annual repayments. This will obviously aid projects with a long life, which might otherwise not appear justified. Many public sector schemes come into this category.

Cost effectiveness

Also in the public sector, it is very often the case that objectives and priorities will have been determined in the political arena. It is then a matter of achieving objectives in the most cost effective way. This has often meant at the least cost in terms of money while taking inadequate account of other factors.

Treatment of intangibles

It is possible to include intangible costs and benefits in calculations of cost effectiveness, albeit with many limitations. The main advantage of doing this, however, is to bring to the attention of policy makers the implicit assumptions of their spending policies. By including both tangible and intangible costs and benefits in the same calculation, an objective method can be found for comparing options. The actual values of the intangibles are only estimates and may be altered by negotiating the values with those affected or those making decisions. Indeed the values are to a large extent arbitrary, but they provide a starting point for discussion. Indeed, there is no reason why the values may not be refined in the light of experience after projects have been completed. It is important to appreciate that the monetary figures provided at this stage are simply the assumptions of a logical deductive argument and not real values in the sense of having a market price which people actually pay.

Capital costs

Of course, it is of little benefit to establish the net present value and the internal rate of return if the project costs remain too great for the resources at the disposal of the client. It is therefore vital to establish the budget and the capital costs of a project before any significant progress can be made. Indeed, it may be necessary for best options to be jettisoned in favour of second or even third best simply on the grounds of capital cost, especially if the client's gearing (the ratio of borrowing to assets) is a constraint.

Budgets are usually determined by factors quite separate from the projects themselves. A retailer's budget might be determined by sales; a government's budget by rates of interest in the economy at large and its policy desire to reduce interest rates; the developer by his credit worthiness. In some cases the budget for the project will in part depend on the nature of the project itself and the willingness of lenders to take risks.

One important feature to be borne in mind at this point is that it is likely that larger projects will have a lower rate of return than smaller ones. It is difficult to maintain a consistently high rate of return on projects. This may at first appear to favour smaller projects. However, as will be seen when funds are allocated to several small projects, it is possible for the rate of return of all the projects taken together to be less than the rate of return on one large venture. There may also be management problems when several small projects are being undertaken instead of one large scheme, which may be in a position to take advantage of economies of scale.

Payback

Probably the most common criterion used to judge proposals is the payback period. This simply estimates the number of years needed to recoup the capital expended on a proposal. It does act as an indicator of the degree of risk attached to any project. The longer money is outstanding the greater the risk is likely to be. It considers only cash flows in future years but does not discount them before adding them together. Nevertheless, many managers like to know the length of time the project will need before beginning to show a positive cash flow, which then contributes to the firm's profits. Clearly, managers will be less keen to invest in projects which only reach this mature stage in the distant future especially if they are hoping for promotion. They will want to demonstrate their own ability to show a quick return on the money they have invested. This criterion will therefore favour those projects with shorter payback periods.

In fact using the payback period as the determining criterion can be most misleading. It takes no account of the life of the project and the fact that money in the future has to be discounted before being aggregated. As a result, it is possible to choose a project with a payback period of four years, which then collapses in the fifth, (the 'time bomb' effect), in preference to a project with a payback period of seven years and an expected life of forty years.

A more sophisticated criterion is the cumulative present value, which calculates the number of years until a project becomes financially viable. The discounted present value of each year's net revenue is accumulated until a positive figure is reached. Thus to begin with, the cumulative present value will be negative as the positive yields, which arise during the building's operational life, are sufficient to compensate for the capital expenditure. However, the sooner this figure becomes positive, the less is the exposure to the risk of financial loss.

Years' purchase

The years' purchase is the factor used to establish how many years it would take to pay for an investment. It is the inverse of the yield. Thus a property with yield of 5 per cent, will take in theory 20 years to recoup its capital purchase price and a property with a yield of 2 per cent would have 50 years' purchase. This of course ignores inflation, which would accelerate the rate of repayment of the principal (the 'principal' being the technical term used to describe the original capital sum used or loaned).

Terminal values

Finally, terminal values may be used as an alternative to discounting back to the present. One alternative is to compound interest rates to some date in the future, namely the year of the decommissioning of the project at the end of its expected useful life. In many ways this has a major advantage in that the progress and performance of the project over its life can be compared to the plan. In calculating terminal values, different interest rates can be easily integrated into the analysis. This overcomes one of the difficulties of the internal rate of return criterion which assumes the internal rate of return is taken to be an average constant interest rate over the life of the project. The calculation of terminal values can be conducted at any point during the life of a project.

four

Initial costs

Introduction

In a recent article, ELLIS and TURNER showed that the areas of highest client dissatisfaction with the services of quantity surveyors (QS) were initial cost advice before the production of drawn information or designs, and cost control of building services.[1] This chapter discusses the importance of early cost estimates, the consequences of error, and the methods which are generally practised. The strengths and weaknesses of each method will be given and it will be argued that more refined methods are required, and these can be made even more useful through the use of computers.

At the outset of a project, a client needs to assess the scale of his financial commitment, likely revenues and expected profits. The overall expenditure will include a wide range of costs. The larger cost items are, normally, land cost and building construction cost. Many of the smaller cost heads, such as professional fees, will be based upon a scale of standard charges. Most are linked to the larger cost headings and can be calculated with confidence once these larger cost items are known. Therefore, the accuracy of the early financial appraisal depends mainly upon how well the construction cost and the revenue income can be forecast.

It is often said that the most important cost report is the first figure that the client hears. This is the one which has the greatest impact, and with which future estimates will be compared despite caveats and qualifications. The accuracy of this preliminary estimate obviously depends upon many complex factors. However, the more accurately the client can anticipate and define his requirements the more reliable will be the preliminary estimate.

Private sector approach

A developer's approach to building projects is similar to an entrepreneur's approach to investment. Both need to make a profit. The developer's profit depends largely on the price paid for the site at the beginning of the project.

Residual land valuation

When land has to be bought for a development, its value to the developer is usually calculated by the residual value method. This method is so called because it shows the amount of money left over for land, after all other costs (including the developer's profits) have been deducted from sales revenue. For example, if a developer plans to sell a building on completion, he may use the following calculation:

	£ m	£ m
Sales		2.6
Building cost	1.14	
Ancillary cost and fees	0.143	
Interest charges	0.19	
Required profit	0.5	
		1.973
Land bid	=	0.627

The developer will usually carry out this method, even if he owns the land, to ascertain whether it would be more profitable to sell it.

In the public sector, local authority housing work in England and Wales has been affected by directives from the Department of the Environment. The financial calculations relating to public housing are similar to the residual valuation formula. The methods are intended to ensure that local authorities work to value for money criteria.

When developing for rental accommodation, the term '*gross development value*' (GDV) is substituted for '*sales*' in the above formula. The GDV is the yearly rental value multiplied by 100/yield percentage. The yield, or the expected anual rate of return upon the investment tends to be between 7 and 9 per cent, depending on market conditions applying to a particular building, rates of interest and inflation. If the client is to be an owner occupier and is required to pay for running costs, then these costs will have to be allowed for.

Methods of budgeting: allocation versus estimation

Budgeting involves setting aside sums of money to pay for future transactions. Thus, the process of budgeting is concerned with predicting expenses. Predictions, according to a recent article in *The Guardian* newspaper, should always be based upon what actually happens in the real world, rather than upon what people think should have happened. Likewise, budgets should be based upon the realistic historical cost analyses rather than on previous budgets.[2] Judgements based on past building costs can be used effectively in estimating costs if adjustments are made for inflation, location and differences in building form, standards and size.

Budgets may be allocated or estimated. The former is where a sum of money is allocated for a purpose with little reference to need or design requirements. The estimation method is where a sum is calculated from a detailed set of needs or requirements. These two extremes are frequently referred to respectively as 'top down' and 'bottom up' approaches.

Top down approaches tend to be inflexible, using, for instance, cost yardsticks. An example of top down budgeting often occurs with local authority annual maintenance budgets, where an amount is allocated for a whole range of maintenance requirements. If this amount is insufficient to deal with those anticipated requirements, the result is that their buildings tend to fall into a state if disrepair until further funding can be found. It would usually be some years before the effects of this strategy emerge. Such effects would probably include premature failure of some components as well as a poor quality building for the users.

One technical solution is therefore to allocate money according to need. This would require the bottom up approach of an analysis of maintenance requirements and costs. However, one difficulty which emerges is that those who decide the annual maintenance budget will not be available to account for effects that emerge 10 or 20 years later.

Thus, while both methods of dealing with maintenance budgets are difficult to control, without checks and safeguards, top down methods will tend to result in shorter term solutions than bottom up approaches. Nevertheless, top down budgeting methods have the following advantages:

1 They are simple to operate and simple to use to control projects. The increased influence of the accountancy profession and current government policies are inclined to top down methods which require less technical expertise and tends to transfer power from architects, engineers

and quantity surveyors to accountants and administrators, who may not have direct contact with the construction industry.

2   They can encourage designers to seek the most economical and efficient design solutions.

3   By providing an upper budget limit, they are appropriate if the client does not trust the discipline or competence of his advisers.

4   They can help to allocate funds on an equitable basis. This is particularly important when allocating funds for works of a social nature, such as community centres or libraries.

The disadvantages of a top down approach are:

1   It is not constructive in decision making. A target is set without reference to the methods used to achieve the objectives. This tends to make the designer's job more difficult than necessary and frequently results in wasted effort.

2   Using a top down approach, it is almost impossible to reconcile the initial expectation of quality with the actual standard achieved. Since the budget is not derived from an assessment of the needs of the building users but from a set of financial constraints, the client is often disappointed with the end result.

3   The aim of increased efficiency and economy frequently results in cutting corners. For example, working to a minimum cost might result in a 'tight fit' design, which cannot be easily adapted and later quickly becomes obsolete. Often, to comply with capital budget constraints, the materials used may have to be of inferior quality with higher maintenance requirements in future years.

4   Top down approaches rely heavily upon statitstics of questionable accuracy. This is particularly true when updating historic costs. Moreover, changing statutory regulations, such as higher standards for earthing requirements or improved insulation also reduce the appropriateness of historical cost data.

To explain, a building cost for a feasibility study is often based on a 'norm' cost, or some statistical basis which is not understood by those who have the greatest control upon the design, namely the client and architect. The architect frequently embarks upon a concept which is bound to exceed the budget. Eventually (often rather late in the design and development process), the quantity surveyor has to present the client with the choice of accepting the design and overspending or cost cutting measures which may include a combination of reducing areas, rationalising shapes and generally lowering specification quality standards.[3] Similar problems also arise in the public sector, where financial managers will also recognise these problems as they appeal against the shortage of funds from central government.[4] In such circumstances, co-operation between members of the construction team tends to become difficult, and people can become very defensive.

Bottom up approach

Using a bottom up approach to budgeting enables the client to use the information for purposes other than merely costing. Since the information must be researched in the first place, it can often also be used for instance, to forecast energy and maintenance running costs. Having explicit information available can help develop more economical designs and reveal opportunities for increased value for money.

A feasibility study, which uses a bottom up approach can make its assumptions explicit. It can therefore be used as a reference point from which design may be discussed, monitored and controlled. If there is some design drift this can be identified and corrected or accepted as preferred at an early stage. By contrast, if a budget is set in a top down manner for, say, a hospital by a cost per bed space, it may be some time before a reliable estimate can be reconciled with the budget.

A major disadvantage of a bottom up approach is the extra time it requires. Furthermore, if a detailed prolonged feasibility study shows the project not to be viable, then the client will have wasted fees and time in which he may have missed a superior opportunity. However, the use of computer cost models can minimise this delay and is discussed in chapter 6.

One of the major objections to operating a bottom up approach to feasibility studies, is that there is a danger that the result becomes a compilation of each consultant's 'wish list'. Each consultant has a view of which items he would like to see included in the section of work for which he is responsible, but would not necessarily be good value from the client's point of view. One reason is that, quite naturally, each consultant sees the aspect for which he has design responsibility, as having greater importance than others may judge to be the case. For example, a mechanical engineer may recommend that for a given office, full variable air volume air conditioning is required, with humidifers. The client, however, might prefer not to pay for such an expensive solution to air treatment. A budget process which simply accepted an engineer's recommendations would often be considered excessive.

In fact, top down methods became favoured by clients partly because they often felt that architects had been too extravagent and that it might have been possible to design a building of a similar quality and appearance for less money. Ideally, bottom up and top down budgeting methods should be synthesised and in practice most methods used are indeed a mixture of both. However, chapters 5 and 6 concentrate on how a bottom up approach to feasibility costing may be developed.

Capital building cost – influences on methods used

Various methods may be used to establish the budget limits of a building project. These will vary depending on the following factors:

1 The nature of the client's experience, competence, size and management structure. Sometimes there is a struggle for power and to influence committees. Where this happens, personnel in one department may wish to wash their hands of the problems of people in other departments. The degree of competence, trust and communication between these levels is critical. Where such difficulties exist, the client often suffers from a lack of analytical feedback and a top down approach is resorted to.

2 The terms of appointment of professional advisers, their competence, attitudes, degree of communication required and levels of co-ordination between them. For instance, if a quantity surveyor is appointed at the recommendation of the architect, there may be a great temptation for him to concede too easily to the architect's wishes and not exercise the control that the client might want. When the quantity surveyor then prepares the budget, he may be tempted to include a little extra for contingencies.

3 Financial constraints on the client. If finance is very limited, a top down approach to the budget is often used.

4 The size, originality and complexity of the project. The larger and more complicated the building the harder it is to estimate construction costs accurately. First of all, the interrelationship between different parts of the building makes it harder to assess the design requirements and costs. Here is an example of the kind of technical problem that might easily arise. If the depth of an office building is 14 m across external walls and the proportion of window to wall is 40 per cent, should some form of air treatment be included, and if so will the storey height module have to be increased? A complicated building may use unusual forms of construction, making it difficult to relate historic cost data to it.

5 The availability of relevant data and experience of the building type.

6 The degree of risk including external factors and matters outside of the control of the design team. Increased risks will justify an extra contingency allowance. The items of major risk should be identified. Frequently, the major risks are related to unforeseeable site conditions.

The stages in the design process

The Royal Institute of British Architects (RIBA) have published a plan of work which describes the stages of design and summarises the duties of the various consultants at each stage.[6] There can be as many as seven stages before a contract may be signed with a builder, namely:

(a) Inception (the original idea and writing a brief)
(b) Feasibility (testing and comparing the economic and financial viability of proposals)
(c) Outline proposals (sketch plans)
(d) Scheme design (completing brief and firming up proposals)
(e) Detail design (working drawings)
(f) Production information (specification of building components)
(g) Bills of Quantities (measurement of a building for costing purposes).

In practice, these stages are often blurred. The impact of computer modelling and CAD will make these stages even harder to distinguish. Nevertheless it remains a useful and well known reference for managing the pre-contract process. Different methods of costing projects are appropriate at different stages.

The inception stage is the point at which the client must decide either to withdraw or proceed further into the feasibility stage. Most clients will be unlikely to form a design team at this point, and consequently they will have limited expertise to draw on. It is at the end of the feasibility stage that the decision whether to proceed with construction will be made.

Cost advice at the inception stage tends to be based on cost per unit, cost per square metre of floor area or cost per cubic metre. The last is difficult to apply and communicate to lay clients, and is generally out of favour with most quantity surveyors.

With the cost per unit methods the unit is a functional unit, such as a cost per bedspace for a hospital, or cost per seat for a theatre. It appears simple to use, but is difficult to adjust accurately should area standards per unit be changed.

The cost per square metre of floor area is the most commonly used single price cost parameter. The method is to multiply an assessed or measured area by a cost per square metre, and then add allowances for external works and contingencies. The gross floor area is the area within external walls, measured over internal walls, stairwells, atria and lift shafts, but excluding open balconies. The main advantage of the cost per square metre (or superficial) method is that all the standard forms of cost analyses show the cost per gross floor area. This facilitates comparison of projects and helps the quantity surveyor to gain expertise in prediction.

Obviously, the accurate use of the superficial method depends upon predicting the area correctly, as well as the cost per square metre. At the inception and often even at the feasibility stage, the sketched or drawn information is too coarse to measure. This may be due to lack of time available, or perhaps because a client brief describing areas of rooms or zones may not yet have been developed.

The shortage of information on intended areas can be overcome by using area analyses which show the breakdown of areas on a previous building of a similar type as shown in figures 4.1 and 4.2.

The effort required to measure the final plans and produce such an analysis is worthwhile if similar buildings are being considered for the future. The uses of such an analysis may include:

1 Compiling the client brief.
2 Estimating the budget.
3 Tendering for cleaning contracts.
4 Allocating maintenance costs where there is more than one user.
5 Using as a basis for future letting contracts.

Cost per unit versus superficial area cost estimating

For most buildings a proportion of their cost is related to their size or area and a proportion is related to the number of units, such as the number of children per class in a primary school. (The size of units will be determined by County Council policy unless the school is private.)

47

NAME - Saffron Walden

DESCRIPTION -	46 sellable flats plus warden, and two guest suites		Areas	% of Gross
1 SELLABLE FLAT AREAS Type A	12 flats at 46.5 m2	:	558	
Type B	18 flats at 48.7 m2	:	877	
Type C & C1	4 flats at 67.4 m2	:	269	
Type D	3 flats at 65.3 m2	:	196	
Type E	4 flats at 65.3 m2	:	261	
Type F	1 flats at 50.7 m2	:	51	
Type G & G1	2 flats at 72.1 m2	:	144	
Type H	2 flats at 65.3 m2	:	131	
SELLABLE AREA TOTAL	46 averaging 54.1 m2 each		2,486	70.1 %
OTHER FLAT AREAS Warden	1 flat at 65.25 m2		65	
Guest suite (ground)	1 flat at 17.78 m2		18	
Guest suite (2nd flr)	1 flat at 20.50 m2		21	

TOTAL OF ALL FLAT AREAS : 2,590 73.0 %
(Includes internal division within flats, but excludes party and corridor walls)

2 ANCILLARY AREAS	Resident's lounge	:	73.3
	Communal kitchen	:	7.8
	Chair store	:	2.7
	Quiet room	:	0.0
	Hairdressing / Chiropody	:	11.1
	Communal launderette	:	16.4
	Communal / disabled toilet	:	4.3
	Warden's office	:	10.8
	Communal and lettable storage	:	41.5
	Refuse / paladin store (outside)	:	0.0
	Wheelchairs	:	0.0
	Service rooms (incl lift motor room)	:	20.4

TOTAL ANCILLARY AREAS : 188.3 5.3 %

3 CIRCULATION	Foyer	:	44.7
	Lift	:	10.0
	Stairs and associated landings	:	119.8
	Corridors, being av. width of 1.50 M. wide)	:	358.6

TOTAL OF COMMUNAL CIRCULATION AREAS : 533.1 15.0 %

4 INTERNAL DIVISION (Calculated from G.F.A. minus above areas) : 237 6.7 %
(Mainly party and corridor walls, only exclusion being walls within flats)

GROSS FLOOR AREA : 3,548

Gross floor area per flat= 72.41 m2
Gross floor area per sellable flat= 77.13 m2

4.1 *Area analysis of an elderly persons group dwelling*

The following items are therefore unit related, being implied by the number of classrooms or pupils: classroom sinks, and other sanitaryware, hot and cold water supplies, waste water plumbing installations and most fixed fittings. To a large extent the cost of certain elements, such as power points and internal doors, will also be largely unrelated to area, since these will depend upon the number of rooms rather than the area of those rooms.

However, for the majority of buildings, by far the greater proportion of their cost will be area related rather than unit related. It follows that if the area can be predicted then the superficial method will be a more accurate measure than the cost per unit method. Furthermore, the superficial method is more constructive to the design team. Nevertheless, familiarity with a building type and the study of relevant cost analyses will help to combine the two methods.

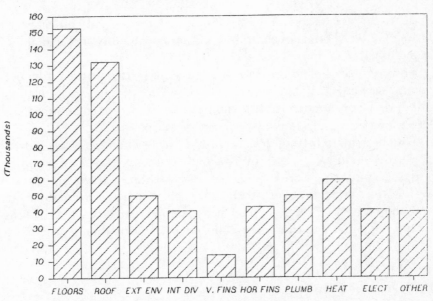

4.2 *Graph of elemental breakdown of a primary school*

Thus, assume that approximately 20 per cent of a primary school's cost is related to the number of pupils and unrelated to area. If area standards were to increase by 10 per cent, then its construction cost can be expected to increase by:

$$\frac{100-20}{100} \times 10\% = 8\%.$$

Feasibility stage

At the feasibility stage, the information becomes more defined and it is appropriate to apply more refined estimating techniques. There are various forms of cost data, used for different purposes and different stages of design. Generally, refined data has been limited to use at the later stages of design, while coarser data, used for the earlier stages has been gained mainly from cost analyses of earlier buildings.

Estimating techniques

Both traditional (or resource) estimating techniques and cost planning techniques, have been advanced by the improved quality and availability of published data and the use of computers.

However, cost planning methods have seen the greater advance, mainly because their techniques are geared to design and budgeting, rather than construction. Cost planning could be described as a means of forecasting and controlling costs for design purposes.

The three main methods of estimating construction costs currently in use in the building industry are builder's estimating, elemental costing and composite rates. Each method is discussed below. These methods may be used in conjunction with each other, particularly elemental costing and composite rates. Price books such as those produced by Griffiths, Laxton, Spon or Wessex are a useful source of information.

Builder's estimating

The builder's estimating or resources method assesses the quantities, time and costs of the resources involved. The builder will not be aware of other contractors' prices in the way that the professional QS will, and therefore his method concentrates on the way that basic costs are generated. This method of costing relates to other functions of the builder's organisation. These functions include management of labour and plant, ordering of materials and bonus payment controls. This method of costing also helps to concentrate the builder's mind on the best methods of construction, how and when to use labour and the efficiency of his use of plant.

The accuracy of this method is as good or bad as the data retrieved from site practice, which means it is often of doubtful accuracy for various reasons. For example, the time taken by labour and plant for various tasks is not normally monitored on site to the level of detail required by the method. The rates per hour for labour and plant are also complicated by matters such as bonus payments applying to some tasks and not to others, and allowances for snagging work. Therefore the cost data used cannot be regarded as true data in any scientific sense, its reliability depending on a degree of interpretation and judgement. To attain high quality cost data would require a degree of thorough on site monitoring and recording of construction activities as described by DEREK BEESTON of the PSA.[7]

Resource estimating is more suited to answering the question: how do we build the design economically? On the other hand, for feasibility and design purposes, the question is: how do we design the building economically? A builder is thus primarily concerned with what peopole do, ie trades or work packages, and their corresponding cost. The client and designer are more concerned with function and its cost, for example, windows let in light and may be compared with other windows, and carpets cover floors and may be compared with vinyl, even though different tradesmen may lay them.

There is a trend towards complete construction of factory finished components with assembly on site rather than on site manufacture and assembly. This is particularly the case with engineering services where the trend is towards total prefabrication of service modules such as plant rooms and even operating theatres for hospitals.[8] This trend will enable the link between people and functioning parts to become closer, as well as encourage simpler lines of legal responsibility for the parts of the building.

The major disadvantage of the resources method for early estimating and cost planning is that it is very difficult to relate the detailed resource costs to the coarse level of information available during the early stages of design. The process of sorting such cost information into a form useful for design is very time consuming and prone to error. Using resource methods also creates a problem of communication. It is unreasonable to expect design teams and clients to think in the technical terms of trades and resources. They talk about walls and doors, not blockwork and first or second fix joinery.

51

Initial Costs

For a client, the use of builder's estimating methods would require not only better cost data, but a closer relationship in the industry between costs and price. A cursory look at figure 4.3 showing cost indices and tender indices demonstrates the very loose relationship between costs and prices. The reality is that sub-contractors and main contractors will try to get the highest acceptable price for a particular job. Savings in costs do not necessarily result in corresponding savings in the price.

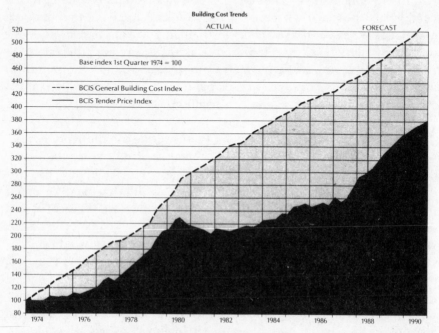

4.3 *Tender and building cost indices.* The Royal Institute of Chartered Surveyors 1988

An advantage of resource estimating is that the estimator acquires a greater understanding of the construction process. A QS in private practice has a major advantage in price estimating over the builder's estimator. The QS knows the prices or rates for many contracts from the bills of quantities of various contractors, whereas the builder only knows his own. The builder's estimator may gain some insight to other contractors' costs by knowing the rates of subcontractors and suppliers who work for other companies as well as their own. The quantity surveyor in private practice may not know the background to the bill rates in terms of labour and plant rates and productivity as well as a builder's estimator. However, for price estimating, this disadvantage is not usually as great as the advantage of knowing various contractors' prices. It is prices, more than costs, which the client is concerned with.

Elemental cost analyses

Elemental cost planning was originally developed by the Department of Education and Science and the form was later adopted by the RICS.[9] Elements are groups of materials and components categorised according to the functional parts of a building. In costing a design, one selects components primarily according to their function. Building elements would therefore be defined as follows:

1 External walls are the interface between inside and outside of the building which does not let in light or objects.

2 External windows are the interface between inside and outside of the building which lets in light.

3 External doors are the interface between inside and outside of the building which can open or close, letting people or objects pass through.

4 Internal walls are the interface between spaces within a building which does not let in light or objects.

5 Internal doors are the interface between spaces within a building which can open or close, letting people or objects pass through.

Although the system has been described as categorising by function, this has to be qualified. Some external walls may have greater thermal or sound resistance than others, and this is part of their function. Similarly, some external walls may be loadbearing, whereas others may hang from the frame.

When an element includes only one component type, the elemental rate is the component rate. However, when the analysis applies to a building which contains a whole variety of components within an element, it becomes difficult to interpret for use in predicting a new project.

It is sometimes argued that experienced professional interpretation of such analyses enables reasonable judgements to be made about the costs of various components included within an element. However, if a roof consists of four types of construction and coverings, then even if one of those constructions is under consideration in a future job, then the analysis cost data on that roof is of very limited use. Its cost would be inaccurate, since it would have been averaged with the three other

ELEMENTAL COST ANALYSIS

Analysis of contract sum	Preliminaries shown separately Costs at tender date		Preliminaries apportioned among elements		Costs at 4th quarter 1988
	Cost/ element £	%	Cost/ element £	Cost/gross floor area £/m²	Cost/gross floor area £/m²
Substructure	36 014	6.13	39 241	32.83	43.73
Superstructure					
Frame	—	—	—	—	—
Upper floors	33 247	5.66	36 226	30.31	40.37
Roof	55 309	9.41	60 264	50.43	67.17
Stairs	9 035	1.54	9 844	8.24	10.97
External walls	58 178	9.90	63 390	53.05	70.66
Windows and external doors	42 878	7.30	46 720	39.10	52.08
Internal walls and partitions	19 237	3.27	20 960	17.54	23.36
Internal doors	28 623	4.87	31 187	26.10	34.76
Group element total	246 507	41.96	268 591	224.76	299.37
Internal finishes					
Wall finishes	15 813	2.69	17 230	14.41	19.19
Floor finishes	20 901	3.56	22 774	19.06	25.39
Ceiling finishes	8 015	1.36	8 733	7.31	9.74
Group element total	44 728	7.61	48 737	40.78	54.32
Fittings and furnishings	17 191	2.93	18 730	15.67	20.87
Services					
Sanitary appliances	9 281	1.58	10 112	8.46	11.27
Services equipment	4 450	0.76	4 849	4.06	5.41
Disposal installations	3 634	0.62	3 960	3.31	4.41
Water installations	6 975	1.19	7 600	6.36	8.47
Heat source	19 962	3.40	21 750	18.20	24.24
Space heating and air treatment	15 339	2.61	16 713	13.99	18.63
Ventilating system	912	0.16	994	0.83	1.11
Electrical installations	17 438	2.97	19 000	15.90	21.18
Gas installations	842	0.14	918	0.77	1.03
Lift and conveyor installations	—	—	—	—	—
Protective installations	1 744	0.30	1 900	1.59	2.12
Communication installations	10 175	1.73	11 087	9.28	12.36
Special installations	—	—	—	—	—
Builder's work in connection with services	8 910	1.52	9 708	8.12	10.82
Builder's profit and attendance on services	6 309	1.07	6 874	5.75	7.66
Group element total	105 971	18.04	115 465	96.62	128.71
Subtotal excluding external works and contingencies	450 411	76.68	490 763	410.68	547.00
External works					
Site works	51 100	8.70	55 679	46.59	62.05
Drainage	27 999	4.77	30 508	25.53	34.00
External services	9 614	1.64	10 475	8.77	11.68
Minor building work	—	—	—	—	—
Group element total	88 713	15.10	96 662	80.89	107.73
Preliminaries	48 302	8.22	–	–	
Totals excluding contingencies	587 426	100.00	587 426	491.57	654.73

4.4 *Print of a conventional elemental cost analysis*

54

specification types. Over the last few decades buildings have become increasingly complex, and elements within buildings have tended to be a mixture of various components. This must certainly be the case when comparing current building practice with most of the prefabricated and 'rationalised' buildings of the 'fifties and 'sixties.

AVERY 1986, states that even when using an elemental cost analysis for a relatively simple factory, ' ... in the absence of a systematic study of rates, the effects of specification and price level remained somewhat confused'.[10] To continue to prepare analyses which are of limited use in prediction, and do little more than help to explain differences after the event, is of doubtful wisdom.

Many of these analyses are still produced manually, but nowadays most computer based bill of quantity production systems incorporate a coding system which enables all bill items in connection with a particular element to have their costs collated according to that element's code. These analyses are not usually used in isolation for prediction, except perhaps for budgeting. However, they provide a good check on the cost plan when the items within it are grouped under the same standard elemental format. Accurate results can be obtained with an experienced interpretation of elemental analyses in conjunction with the bills of quantities, but the interpretation required means that the process is far less definitive than a design team would require.

Composite rates: assembling

Composite rates are the most common method of estimating and cost planning used by quantity surveyors. Other terms used for this approach are approximate quantities or components. This method is the most useful for designers working closely with quantity surveyors, as it is sufficiently definitive without being too unwieldy. The method tends to be used in conjunction with elemental analyses. Elemental cost planning involves grouping component costs within their elemental categories.

Various methods are currently practised for costing these components. The most common technique is to measure, for each component, all the items of work in connection with it. For a traditional strip wall foundation, for instance, this would include: excavation, earthwork support, level and compact, backfill, cart-away, concrete, brickwork and damp proof coursing. This method has the advantage of being in wide use, and the quantity surveyor experienced in it will increase both the speed of preparation and the accuracy of his estimate.

Like the other methods of costing, costing components also entails certain problems. These are as follows:

1 The accuracy of this method depends largely upon the assumptions that the QS makes in buiding up the rates from priced bills. For example, to estimate the cost of a cantilevered balcony at sketch scheme stage requires assumptions to be made about the quality, quantity of steel and other items needed, and these assumptions may in fact be reversed when the detailed design is carried out.

2 It is impractical for an architect to check the detailed but important assumptions made by a QS in his costing. From the architect's point of view, the method of costing is too detailed and does not relate to the way he described his ideas, which he does more effectively by relating them to a previous building. This method therefore relies to a large extent upon the intuition of the QS.

3 Assembling costs takes time. Frequently, by the time the information is firm enough to estimate with confidence, it is too late to make major changes in the design.

4 Cost analyses of tenders are very often too crude to enable judgements to be made on any errors made when predicting costs.

In practice, component rates for one job may be adapted for others, and the QS office may hold a library of useful component rates in readiness for cost planning work. However, it is important that the architect and QS have a common understanding of what the rates represent and what alternatives there may be.

FERRY[11] describes a practical way of preparing amplified cost analyses down to the component level. Although his techniques were encouraged by the Royal Institution of Chartered Surveyors, they were too time consuming for the vast majority of practices. However, the improved performance and lower prices of computers in recent years have enabled a variant on his method to become more viable. Chapter 5 explains this approach further.

Each of the above methods has advantages and disadvantages. Flexibility is called for to make the best use of the data from whatever source. Frequently a detailed estimate may be built up primarily using the component costing method and then checked against elemental cost plans. Typically, most of the component costs will be assembled from rates in bills of quantities with unusual items priced from basic resources, such as manufacturers' or suppliers' price lists.

An interactive approach

For many clients, the formation of the right design team is the first important step in a feasibility study. The team will depend upon the type and complexity of the project but typically, for an office project, will include the architect, quantity surveyor, structural engineer, mechanical engineer and electrical engineer. If the office is to be rented, then a letting agent may be included. A modern office which uses extensive communication cabling for video links, computers and telephones may justify the inclusion of an *information technology* (IT) consultant in the design team.

It is vital to create a teamwork approach for efficient project management, more specifically to engender a spirit of mutual trust, respect and understanding between members of a construction team. Unfortunately, some architects may not be willing to enter into a value management exercise which they see as undermining their position. Likewise, not all consultants will be open and constructive in their contributions to such an exercise. Effective cost planning can be very difficult if consultants are required to make their judgements explicit, any errors being exposed.

When each consultant's fee is linked to the value of his part of the building work on a percentage basis, each consultant has to compete for a 'slice of the cake', creating an adversarial approach to project management. Where the design fees are 'all in' for the whole team this can help overcome inherent devisiveness, and allow some flexibility in apportioning fees based on each consultant's own time and resources spent working on a project.

The failure of good working relations between consultants can have costly repercussions. One example of the failure of teamwork may serve to illustrate the point. The design team in a particular local authority decided to cost plan a school and look at alternative specification standards. The QS argued that if double glazing were used, reductions could be made in the size of the heat source and emitters, and even a slight saving on the size of the boiler room. The architect and mechanical engineer argued on the other hand, that this would be unwise, because if the scheme were to exceed the budget, the double glazing would be one of the first things to be cut from the scheme to make savings and the heating would be undersized as a result.

The QS, whose function is to enforce savings, if required, would probably not consider that the heating system might be undersized as a result, and would not be willing to take responsibility if the resulting heating system were inadequate. The need for such savings is understandable, as the strict financial controls placed upon local government by central government allows very little of the flexibility which the private sector enjoys.

Energy saving measures, such as improved insulation, may often be viable only if the theoretic reductions in heat capacity requirements and initial costs are made explicit. To effect savings, the engineer is required to do extra work, cutting the cost of the heating system and therefore his own fees. He has no incentive to co-operate with the rest of the team.

However, not all projects need suffer from this lack of incentive on the part of the consultants. For instance, a successful teamwork approach was adopted when Thamesdown Borough Council conducted a feasibility study for civic offices in Swindon. A shopping list of alternative components was drawn up between the QS and the architect. (Building components are forms of construction such as softwood double glazed stained windows or concrete interlocking tiles on 38 mm by 25 mm battens on roofing felt.) With the help of the various consultants, each component was then costed and multiplied by the quantity, calculated by a computer cost model.

One of the choices was whether to select a steel or concrete framed structure. Initially, steel appeared to be the more cost effective, since steel frames are lighter than concrete. Moreover, because the ground conditions were thought to be poor in the area, a steel frame would enable savings to be made on piling costs.

A very enlightening meeting was held with all the consultants present. A new soil report showed the ground to be far better than expected and a revised piling cost for both the steel frame and concrete frame solutions were produced. Following the revised soil report, the first changes made on the cost model were that the choices for both frame and piles were changed from steel to concrete.

The decision to change to a concrete frame rather than steel, raised the cost of the frame slightly but this was more than offset by savings in other parts of the building. The reduction in the size of downstand beams enabled the storey height to be reduced whilst maintaining the clear height. The areas and costs of the vertical elements and wall finishes reduced automatically. A spray applied finish on to the concrete was substituted for suspended ceilings, and uplighters substituted for conventional fluorescent lamps. The cooling load was assessed to be less because of the heavier structure and higher thermal inertia (slower response to outside temperatures), and therefore the required capacity and cost were reduced. Judgements were made in a collective interactive way, with each consultant scanning the options and checking the design and cost effects upon the elements for which he was responsible. This meeting took about an hour, and although it was followed up by a certain amount of checking, the result was a meaningfully agreed budget based upon a solution to which all consultants had contributed. It is difficult to imagine the sort of judgements, interactions and general method of working in the above example without the use of a computer.

Conclusion

An inflexible *top down* budgeting system simplifies financial planning. Confidence in a budget is necessary when attracting funding, looking at the viability of a project, or assessing land values. However, if a budget is fixed, then any inaccuracy in setting it is likely to result in adjustments to standards and areas.

The main advantage of a flexible *bottom up* approach to budgeting is the need to understand the elements which together form the building, because the bottom up approach focuses attention on the individual components.

The overriding requirement of good prediction is good analysis of, and feedback from completed buildings. Feedback may take the form of cost analyses, area analyses and debriefings at the end of contracts.

Computers may be used with more refined cost information for cost planning and budgeting at an earlier stage of design than has been practical in the past. Techniques using computers can assist the client to define, develop and cost his requirements at the feasibility stage. So far, however, computers have been used mainly to computerise existing techniques. They have, nevertheless, opened up opportunities which were previously not possible or viable. These opportunities are explained in the following chapters.

References

[1] ELLIS, C and A TURNER, (1986), Procurement Problems, *Chartered Quantity Surveyor*, April 1986 p 11.
[2] CORNES, RALPH, (1986), 'Why systems need a real life analysis', *The Guardian* 20 March 1986 p 17.
[3] RAFFERTY, J, (1987), 'The state of Cost/Price Modelling in the UK Construction Industry. A Multicriteria Approach', in Brandon, PS, editor, *Building Cost Modelling and Computers*, Spon.
[4] *The Guardian*, 'Simple Maths', editorial of 22 September 1988 p 22.

[5] Editorial News 'Users blamed for PSA Overspend', *Arthitects' Journal* 10 August 1988.

[6] RIBA (1973), *Plan of work for design team operation*, Royal Institute of British Architects, London.

[7] BEESTON, D, (1987), 'A future for cost modelling', in Brandon, P S, editor, *Building Cost Modelling and Computers*, Spon.

[8] BERRY, J, (1987), 'Cinderella no Longer', *Architects' Journal* 'Focus', September 1987 p 22.

[9] DES Building Bulletin 4: cost study. HMSO 1972.

[10] AVERY, DW, (1987), 'Steps Towards Cost Modelling for the Control Small Factory Build Cost', *Building Cost Modelling and Computers*, Spon.

[11] FERRY, DR, (1973), *Cost Planning of Buildings*.

[12] CARTLIDGE, D and I MEHRTENS, (1982), *Practical Cost Planning: guide for surveyors and architects*, Hutchinson Educational.

five

Costing components

Introduction

In the United Kingdom there are, broadly speaking, two types of building cost studies, namely *cost planning studies* and *cost analyses*. Cost planning is used to predict and control costs, while a cost analysis is a cost report of the tender, submitted by the building contractor employed to carry out the work. The cost analysis is used as the feedback or post-mortem of the cost plan.

Using component costing techniques, as described in chapter 4, for cost planning in feasibility studies leads to a mismatch between the form of data for prediction and that obtained from cost analysis. This is because the conventional elemental cost breakdown works at a coarser level of detail than the final analysis.

If the component quantities approach is to be used effectively in feasibility studies, it is necessary to develop a system of analysis, which supplies cost data at the same level of detail as the cost plan, using the same methods of measurement throughout. Such cost information would be most helpful used in conjunction with cost modelling techniques at an early stage of design. These techniques will be described in chapter 6.

In this chapter the elemental costing system is developed to provide component and element rates in one operation. The use of a detailed analysis of costs should achieve more accurate predictions than the traditional methods described in chapter 4. However, the successful use of the methods advocated here depends on clients and consultants adopting a broad view so that the effort and data generated is put to maximum use.

Consistent cost information

Cost information should contain the following characteristics:

1 It should allow for the same form of costing at all stages of the design process.

2 It must communicate meaningfully to designers and clients.

3 Component costs should be grouped within their elements, so that costs may be inspected at a broad or more detailed level as required.

4 Cost categories should be as close to existing methods as possible, to make use of existing cost data and expertise.

5 Cost items should enable comparisons to be made with other items within the same element group to aid the selection of components.

6 It should avoid technical jargon as much as possible.

7 For specialist areas, such as lighting, the methods of costing should follow closely, or at least be reconcilable with the method of estimating used by the particular design consultant.

8 It should use similar descriptions and methods of measurement in the calculation of both initial costs and costs-in-use for *life cycle costing* (LCC).

9 Cost information should be relatively inexpensive to collect.

Consistent cost models and cost data will tend to improve communication and facilitate the reconciliation of costs from one stage in the design process to the next. This will help to control costs within budget and pinpoint the effects of a design drifting from the original on which the feasibility study was based.

In the early stages of the design of all but the simplest buildings there can be a problem of information saturation.[1] Too much information can be as harmful as insufficient or incomplete data. Moreover, there is little point in using a cost model if the design team do not understand its output. It is necessary for all the consultants, but particularly for the cost planner and architect, that the number of variables they have to deal with, is not excessive. A research paper published in 1981 by Reading University suggested that a cost plan which struck the right balance between accuracy, effort required, and communication would include about 100 items.[2]

On average one hundred component items appears to be a reasonable number of variables in building cost planning. The same form of costing may be used for different projects, where appropriate. This will allow all those involved with a building project to learn from their experience. Moreover, component costs taken from one job may be adjusted and applied to others. In new building work at Thamesdown Borough Council, the component costing method of cost planning the number of different types of components varied from about 60 categories for simple bungalows to about 160 for large civic offices project.

Comparison and common denominators

Costing a building proposal enables designers to see what alternatives may exist. The elemental costing format illustrated in figure 5.1 shows cost information in terms of function rather than material construction, since the purpose is to evaluate the benefits derived from expenditures.[3] Data for environmental services elements is less obvious and is explained later on in this book.

Minimum jargon

Various building professionals need to communicate on common terms. For most components in a building there is no great problem. It is reasonably clear what 'standard double glazed stained softwood windows' are. However, such descriptions do not define the component precisely, and ideally the cost should be refined if, for example, there is an unusually high proportion of opening lights. The idea is that the terms used in early cost advice correspond to the language of the design team in the early stages of design. It is at the early stages that such cost guidance can be of greatest benefit. To aim for precise definitions at the early stages would burden those involved with too many questions and more information than can be assimilated by the design team in a limited time.

Frequently the terms discussed in consultants' meetings range from one extreme of meaningless statistics and vagueness, to another of precise jargon, which others do not understand. This is often done to avoid scrutiny by the other consultants! Consultants may also be unwilling to give away some of their hard won specialist expertise.

The following example of lighting design may demonstrate the above point. An electrical engineer may suggest that the cost per square metre for lighting and associated circuitry for a particular building should be about £30 per square metre of floor area. Alternatively, he may suggest a provisional schedule of luminaire fittings, perhaps even identified by catalogue numbers. At the feasibility stage it is best to agree upon the fundamentals, using terms which may be understood and agreed by the team.[3]

EXTRACT OF ELEMENT / COMPONENT COST PLAN

Element and Cost	Cost/m2 G.F.A.	Element Rate	Sub-Element	Calc Qty	Enter % for Specification Choice	Component, or specification choice.	Unit Quantity	Unit Rate	Total Cost of Spec Choice
FLOOR FINISHES 7,953	22.63	23.78	BASE LAYERS	335 M2		50mm screed on insitu concrete floor.(Uninsulated)	M2	5.32	
			(Ground= 111.5 M2)		33	65mm cement / sand screed on synthaprufe on p.c.floor	112 M2	11.90	1,327
			(Upper= 223.0 M2)			Flooring grade moisture resistant chipboard on 50mm. polystyrene insulation.	M2	10.12	
					67	65mm cement / sand screed on sound insulating quilt on suspended p.c.floor.	223 M2	9.89	2,206
						Flooring grade moisture resistant chipboard on 50mm. polystyrene insulation on levelling screed	M2	10.73	
			FINISH	335 M2		Vinyl tiles.	M2	6.93	
						Vinyl sheet.	M2	10.86	
						Vinyl seamless sheet safety flooring E.g. "Altro"	M2	26.47	
					82	"Lady Arabella" or similar man-made fibre carpet.	273 M2	9.02	2,466
					10	"Ploter" or similar man-made fibre carpet.	33 M2	13.16	440
			(Note: All hessian-backed with separate rubber underlay, so no foam-backed carpets must be used).		8	"Contour" or similar man-made fibre carpet.	28 M2	19.89	549
						Carpet of mainly wool, approx 80% to 20% mix	M2	41.84	
						Cork tiles	M2	28.09	
						Ceramic tiles.	M2	36.88	
						Quarry tiles.	M2	133.17	
						Mats and matwells	M2		
			SKIRTINGS	423 M.	100	S.W.	423 M.	2.28	964
						H.W.	M.	2.73	
						Welded vinyl	M.	4.73	
						Quarry or ceramic tiles.	M.	6.51	

CEILING FINISHES 13.42	14.09 TO ROOF OR HOUSE FLOORS	112 M2	92 S.w. noggins between ceiling joists.	102 M2	2.91	297
4,714	BASES > TO FLOORS BETWEEN FLATS	223 M2	3 Plugging and battening to p.c. beam and pot floors	6 M2	5.24	32
	(Battening has to incorporate void for ventilation ducting).		89 Screw, pack out and batten to p.c. widespan floors	198 M2	6.58	1,306
	FINISH	335 M2	9.5mm wallboard & artex finish.	M2	4.65	
			92 13mm wallboard & artex finish.	307 M2	5.54	1,699
			13mm wallboard with 5mm skim and emulsion.	M2		
	(Usually used in circulation areas, }		8 Suspended "lay in" 600 x 600 grid fissured ceiling	28 M2	12.87	355
	and no need for a base }		Higher quality concealed grid suspended ceiling	M2	15.14	
	OVER BALCONY OR WALKWAY	M2	100 19mm ply boarding to external ceiling	M2	25.12	
			19mm masterboard or similar to external ceiling	M.	7.96	
	COVING	450 M.	100 Gyproc or similar coving.	450 M.	2.28	1,024
	(Excludes within corridor)		Moulded coving	M.		
FIXED FITTINGS 27.41	1,606 KITCHEN FITTINGS	6 SETS	100 Kitchen fittings:-B.D.C.cabinets: "Henly" or similar	6 SETS	698.26	4,190
9,633	COOKERS	6 NR	100 Electric fan oven with hood and sealed hot plate.	6 NR.	425.20	2,551
	(Cost to include associated electrical work)			NR.		
(Calc both sides of corridors)	HANDRAILS TO CORRIDORS	36 M.	Handrails to corridors	M.	28.00	
(Assume 1.00 / flat) >	WARDROBES	6 NR	100 Built-in "Panavista" mirror fronted wardrobes.	6 NR	219.63	1,318
	SHELVES	6 SETS	100 Slatted shelving to airing cupboards.	6 FLAT	80.07	480
	SUNDRY IRONMONGERY	6 SETS	100 Grab rails, h & c hooks, mirrors etc.	6 FLAT	62.41	374
	FIRE EXTINGUISHERS	6 SETS	100 Fire extinguishers.	6 FLAT	74.56	447
	PELMET & CURTAIN BATTENS	6 SETS	100 Pelmets and curtain battens	6 FLAT	17.08	102
	TOWEL RAILS	6 NR.	100 Heated.	6 NR.	28.37	170
	(Assumes 1 per bath plus 1 per shower)		Unheated.	NR.		

5.1 Extract of elemental/component cost plan

Use of common data for various purposes

An important aim of information technology systems is that information gathered for one purpose can be used for another. In computing science and data processing, this is an important aspect of what is known as *relational database theory*. In many industries, people are striving to find compatible forms of data which have many uses. Frequently, many of the uses are often not even imagined during the original development work.

Unfortunately, in the construction industry various consultants may measure the same building for different reasons, when one set of measurements and descriptions might have been meaningful to all. The starting point needs to be the definition of data, rather than the way calculations will use such data. In future is will be the ease and ability to generate, maintain and retrieve good quality data in a data bank, which will determine the viability of computer systems, rather than the ease in developing applications for its use.

It would, of course, be possible to establish a form of such cost data, which could be applied to many different files and applications. The main obstacle to achieving this is not technical; it is whether people in one department or design discipline are prepared to help another department or design discipline, and whether they realise that such sharing of information is possible.[4]

Entities not activities

Relational databases work most effectively with very simple descriptions for each item or entity. Entities (meaning tangible objects) are used in computing science rather than processes or activities.[5] Using computers, cost data is therefore related to physical components and their implied functions rather than to the cost of activities, which are hard to monitor and maintain. Moreover, the costing of construction activities as carried out by a contracts surveyor for a builder does not relate to other applications, such as energy forecasting.

Environmental services

Energy consumption forms a significant proportion of a building's running cost. Energy use is a difficult item to forecast accurately, partly because it is so dependent upon the way the building is used. It is especially difficult to forecast in the early stages of design. However, for each of the components which make up the external elements of a building, we can associate a U-value, which is the measure of its thermal resistance. The lower the U-value, the greater is its resistance, or conversely, the lower its thermal conductivity. The formula for the U-value = 1/sum of the resistances of the separate materials within the component. The resistances must include the surfaces and interfaces between the materials as well as the materials themselves. This implies the inclusion of small resistances at the face of the glass of a window, and at the faces of the bricks and blocks in an external wall.[6]

We can also associate a corresponding Y-value, which is a measure of a component's thermal weight or inertia. This will depend mainly upon the component's mass but also upon the specific heat of the materials within it. This property is generally less critical than the U-value. However, for an intermittently used building (such as a primary school), a lower thermal inertia will help reduce the heat load for the warm up period. In buildings such as offices, this factor will have a major effect upon a building's inclination to overheat, the heat sink effect. It is therefore an important factor in evaluating cooling design loads and running costs. Unfortunately it is rare that this difference is considered when the choice is made between a heavy concrete or a lighter steel framed building.

The computer calculated energy program is co-ordinated with the initial cost calculations by using the same form of component measurement and calculated quantities as are used for costing purposes. An energy forecasting model will have much in common with a heating design model. The same model can therefore be used for both purposes. The link between the costing model and energy and heating design model enables a QS to find cost effective solutions, taking into account both services design and running costs.[7]

The cost of the lighting installation in a building is harder to predict at the feasibility stage than the cost of the heating system. The quantity of artificial lighting required depends on information about the building, which will not emerge until later in the design process. However, this difficulty may be lessened using the formulae below.

Lumen is the measure of quantity of light output and equates to kW for heating. *Lux* is the measure of illuminance or brightness at a surface and is equivalent to temperature for heating. In the client brief, it is the lux level (at least) that should be specified. The *maintenance factor* is an allowance for dust and dirt that build up on light fittings, reducing their output as well as the natural reduction in lumen output of the fitting over its life. The assessment of the *utilisation factor* for lighting at an early stage is

67

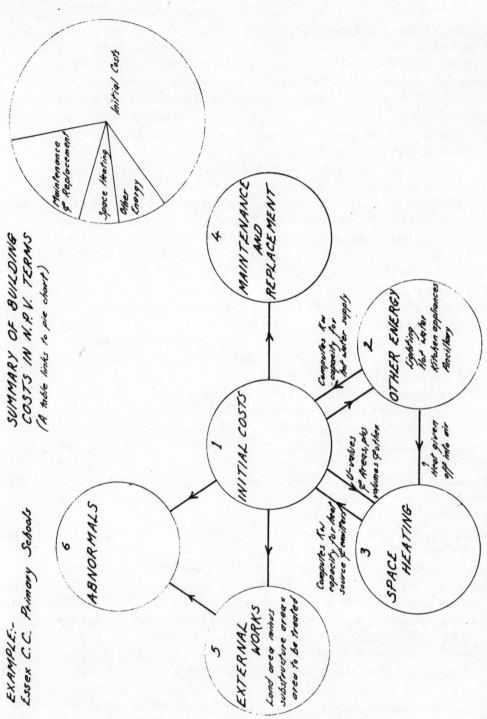

EXAMPLE:-
Essex C.C. Primary Schools

SUMMARY OF BUILDING
COSTS IN N.P.V. TERMS
(A table links to pie chart)

5.2 *Flow chart of Essex CC school LCC system*

difficult, since it measures the loss of light from light fittings to the plane at which the lux level is to be achieved. Its precise calculation depends upon size and shape of rooms and reflectances of surfaces. Unfortunately, this cannot be measured until long after the feasibility stage. However, a competent electrical engineer should be in a position to assess a likely range of utilisation factors. Later in the design process, this should be reviewed and firmed up in conjunction with the choice of light fittings and the reflectances and colour of ceiling and wall finishes.

The formula, then, for total lumens required is:

$$L = \frac{A \times l}{m \times u} \text{ where } L = \text{total lumens}$$
$$A = \text{area}$$
$$l = \text{lux level}$$
$$m = \text{maintenance factor}$$
$$u = \text{utilisation factor}$$

To find the likely number of fittings, divide L by the average lumens output per fitting.

An example will serve to illustrate the method. Assume an office of 1,000 square metres with a ceiling of 70 per cent reflectance and wall surfaces of 50 per cent reflectance. From this information an engineer might advise that utilisation and maintenance factors of 0.52 and 0.80 respectively should be used. If the client requires an illuminance level of 500 lux and if the architect and electrical engineer have decided that the great majority of fittings will be 1.8 m long fluorescent luminaires with opaque diffusers emitting 5,800 lumens each, then the number of fittings can be calculated as follows:

$$\text{Let } L = \text{total lumens}$$
$$A = 1,000 \text{ sq m}$$
$$l = 500 \text{ lux}$$
$$m = 0.80$$
$$u = 0.52$$

Substituting in formula above:

$$L = \frac{1,000 \times 500}{0.80 \times 0.52}$$

$$= 1,201,923$$

If the average lumens per fitting is 5,800, then:

$$\text{Total number of fittings required} = \frac{1,201,923}{5,800}$$

$$= 207 \text{ fittings}$$

It is usually appropriate to add some tolerance for odd corners which may be awkward to illuminate, so say 230 number fittings. Engineers should then be in a better position to assess the electrical load of the building, the heating gain for assessing cooling requirements and even running costs.[8]

Energy for lighting can account for as much as 80 per cent of the energy cost in a commercial building.[9] It is possible to make a reasonable forecast of the energy consumption for lighting by linking each lighting choice with a corresponding figure for its energy efficiency or efficacy, measured as the lumen output per watt consumed.

Continuing with the lighting example above, assume now that the number of hours the lights are switched on per year is expected to be 800 hours, with an efficacy of 70 lumens per watt and on-peak electricity at 6.1 pence per kWhr, the calculation of energy costs from lighting alone would then be as follows:

$$\frac{230 \times 5,800 \times 800}{70 \times 1000} \times \frac{6.1}{100} = \pounds 93$$

Some of the heat given off by the lights will usefully supplement the heat requirement, but may increase any cooling loads. A co-ordinated energy model should take account of this.

Maintenance

One could make a better assessment of the costs of future planned maintenance requirements, by associating each component with its maintenance requirements over time. For example, a brick and block cavity wall may be repointed every 20 years at a current cost of £14 per square metre. Again, having established the capital cost of a sectional gas boiler of a specified size, the seasonal efficiency (as opposed to the efficiency under design conditions) may be estimated at approximately 72 per cent. While it may require to be serviced every year, the burners may need to be replaced about every eight years and the whole boiler and flue replaced after 20 years.[10] For lighting, we can associate a corresponding anticipated bulb life for each type of fitting and lamp.

An excellent source of information on the maintenance periods and life expectancy of components is *Maintenance Cycles and Life of Building Components and Materials* published by the National Building Agency Construction Consultants.[11] This does not include costs. However, a useful source of maintenance costs is the Building Cost Information Service, *Building Maintenance Price Book* 1989.[12]

The following example is taken from a computer program written using the *Lotus 1-2-3* spreadsheet program. It enables very quick sensitivity analyses, allowing the user to test the effect of changing mathematical variables in the program. Such variables might include the discount rate, the life of the building, or the maintenance periods and lives of some of its components.

If life cycle costing is to be useful, then it must be effective even in the early stages of design, when decisions taken will affect the operation of the building over its entire useful existence. By adopting consistent forms of description and measurement of components, it is possible to use feasibility studies at the earliest stages of decision making affecting a design proposal. Thereafter, the same figures may be used as a basis for monitoring and managing the building throughout its life.

Methods of generating capital cost data

The main methods used by independent firms of quantity surveyors to generate cost data are firstly to analyse previous tenders to the elemental level and secondly to compile component rates. This means that to carry out a comprehensive analysis requires two separate processes for one set of costings or priced bill.

Bills of quantities are lists of items of finished work used and it can be difficult to relate these to the components and elements accurately. This is a major cause of error in the preparation of cost analyses unless codes are assigned to components prior to measuring for the bills of quantities. The codes should then appear in these bills. These codes may also be used in the cost model, the last cost check of the design, and the cost library. The design, maintenance and use of a cost library is discussed further in chapter 10.

In the process of measuring a building, all items in connection with a particular component are given the same code, corresponding to drawing details, such as the eaves, verges, and external doors. When the bill of quantities is priced by the contractor, the rates of each item are entered into the computer and a check upon the compilation of the bill is

EXTRACTS OF MAINTENANCE AND REPLACEMENT COSTS
****

	Enter:
Enter life of building:	40
Enter period at end of life at which replacement will cease	5
Enter average medium term rate of interest for investment	12.0 %
Enter percentage average long term inflation rate:-	6.0 %
so net discount rate, (calculated)= 6.0 %	
Enter index for maintenance price rates basis	340

Descriptions:-	QUANTITY (informed by cost model)	Treatment	MAINTENANCE / SERVICING				OBSOLESCENCE / REPLACEMENT					TOTAL NET PRESENT VALUES
			Years Inter-val	Unit Rate	Present Values	Hours life (where applicable)	Perc-entage replaced	Years Inter-val	Unit Rate	Present Values	Hours life (where applicable)	
S.w.double glazed windows (oil gloss painted)	10.0 M2	Prep,clean, & 2 cts oil	4	6.42	214		15	30	177	46		325
S.w.double glazed windows (stained)	10.0 M2	Clean & Stain	6	7.65	160		15	25	170	59		285
Hardwood double glazed windows or screens (E.g. bays)	10.0 M2	Clean & Stain	4	7.65	256		15	40	227	0		320
Tungsten	43.0 LAMPS	bulb	0.70		442	850	100	4.13	9	1,148	5,000	1,590
Flourescent	12.0 LAMPS	starter & lamp	2.64	3.40	200	4,000	100	7.92	40	683	12,000	883
Off-peak storage heaters (kWHrs storage per flat = 26.43 kWHrs)	6 FLATS	Yearly service	1	21.25	1,893		100	20	26	1,261		3,154

MAINTENANCE TOTAL:= 3,166

REPLACEMENT TOTAL:= 3,198

TOTAL FUTURE MAINTENANCE/REPLACEMENT FOR ALL 6 FLATS IN THIS MODEL = 6,558

SO PER FLAT = 1,093

EXTRACTS OF MAINTENANCE AND REPLACEMENT COSTS
****

Enter:

Enter life of building: 60 (CHANGED FROM 40)
Enter period at end of life at which replacement will cease: 5
Enter average medium term rate of interest for investment: 10.0 % (CHANGED FROM 12%)
Enter percentage average long term inflation rate:- 6.0 %
so net discount rate, (calculated)= 4.0 %

Enter index for maintenance price rates basis: 340

Descriptions:-	QUANTITY (informed by cost model)	Treatment	MAINTENANCE / SERVICING				OBSOLESCENCE / REPLACEMENT					TOTAL NET PRESENT VALUES
			Years Inter-val	Unit Rate	Present Values	Hours life (where applicable)	Perc-entage replaced	Years Inter-val	Unit Rate	Present Values	Hours life (where applicable)	
S.w.double glazed windows (oil gloss painted)	10.0 M2	Prep,clean, & 2 cts oil	4	6.42	336		15	30	177	82		499
S.w.double glazed windows (stained)	10.0 M2	Clean & Stain	6	7.65	254		15	25	170	132		468
Hardwood double glazed windows or screens (E.g. bays)	10.0 M2	Clean & Stain	4	7.65	400		15	40	227	71		553
Tungsten	43.0 LAMPS	bulb	0.70	0.50	659	850	100	4.13	9	1,827	5,000	2,486
Flourescent	12.0 LAMPS	starter & lamp	2.64	3.40	303	4,000	100	7.92	40	1,104	12,000	1,406
Off-peak storage heaters	6 FLATS	Yearly service	1	21.25	2,847		100	20	26	2,688		5,534

(kWHrs storage per flat = 26.43 kWHrs)

MAINTENANCE TOTAL:= 4,798   REPLACEMENT TOTAL= 5,902

TOTAL FUTURE MAINTENANCE/REPLACEMENT FOR ALL 6 FLATS IN THIS MODEL = 10,946

SO PER FLAT = 1,824

5.3 *Extract of maintenance program*

EXTRACT OF AMPLIFIED COST ANALYSIS

Element and cost	Cost/M2 G.F.A.	Element Rate	Sub-Element	Code	Specification Choice	Unit Quantity	Unit Rate	Cost of Sub-Element
WALL FINISHES 49,613	19.94	6.83	TO PERIMETER OF FLATS	18.A. 2	Uninsulated dry lining (using plaster dabs)	5,119 M2	6.33	32,420
			TO WALLS WITHIN FLAT	18.B. 1	1 p.& 2 coats of emulsion on gyproc stud partitions.	1,216 M2	1.20	1,460
				4	Medium quality coloured ceramic tiles.	116 M2	21.93	2,544
				5	High quality ceramic tiles.	560 M2	22.69	12,708
			COMMUNAL AREAS	18.D. 2	Wallpaper (at P.C. £6/roll at Jan 88 prices)	91 M2	3.00	273
				3	Emulsion on fair faced block (Provisional).	166 M2	1.25	208
FLOOR FINISHES 55,174	22.17	23.37	BASE LAYER,GROUND FLOOR	19.A. 2	Flooring grade moisture resistant chipboard on 25mm polystyrene	956 M2	7.81	7,471
			BASE LAYER,UPPER FLOORS	19.B. 1	Flooring grade moisture resistant chipboard on 50mm polystyrene	1,341 M2	8.41	11,274
			FINISH	19.C. 3	"Altro" vinyl seamless sheet safety flooring	85 M2	20.15	1,713
				4	"Lady Arabella" jute backed nylon carpet	1,599 M2	11.30	18,069
				5	"Nova" nylon carpet (To kitchen areas).	183 M2	6.53	1,195
				6	"Contour" carpet, (to communal circulation areas).	333 M2	16.33	5,438
				7	Higher quality carpet of mainly wool, approx 80% to 20% mix	149 M2	35.10	5,230
				8	Cork tiles	4 M2	23.75	95
				9	Mats and matwells	8 M2	78.50	628
			SKIRTINGS	19.D. 1	S.W.	1,925 M	2.11	4,062

CEILING FINISHES 9.35 10.07
23,276

Element	Code	Description	Qty	Unit	Rate	Amount
BASE TO TOP STOREY	20.A. 1	S.w. noggins between ceiling joists at 450mm centres	829	M2	3.26	2,700
BASE TO UPPER FLOORS	20.B. 1	Plugging and battening to underside of beam & pot p.c. floor	1,164	M2	4.26	4,962
FINISH	20.C. 1	9.5mm wallboard & artex finish.	979	M2	3.70	3,624
	2	13mm wallboard & artex finish.	1,014	M2	4.54	4,606
	5	Suspended "lay in" 600 x 600 grid fissured ceiling	259	M2	10.27	2,661
	6	Higher quality recessed grid suspended ceiling	60	M2	12.79	768
COVING	20.E. 1	Gyproc or similar coving.	2,197	M	1.80	3,955

FIXED FITTINGS 21.83 1,874
54,339

Element	Code	Description	Qty	Unit	Rate	Amount
KITCHEN FITTINGS	21. 1	Kitchen fittings:-B.D.C.cabinets: "Henly" range	29	Sets	781.34	22,659
COOKERS	2	Ariston fan oven with hood and sealed hot plate.	29	Nr	462.28	13,406
WARDROBES	5	Built-in "Panavista" mirror fronted wardrobes.	30	Nr	229.10	6,873
SHELVES	6	Slatted shelving to airing cupboards.	30	Nr	56.57	1,697
SUNDRY IRONMONGERY	7	Sundry ironmongery, grab rails, h & c hooks, mirrors etc.	30	Flats	71.47	2,144
FIRE EXTINGUISHERS	8	Fire extinguishers.	30	Flats	95.70	2,871
PELMETS & CURTAIN BATTENS	9	Pelmets and curtain battens	30	Flats	19.63	589
	R	Equipment for, laundry, chiropody and hairdressing. (Prov. sum)	1	ITEM	2,500	2,500
	R	Entrance feature and hatch to office. (Prov. sum).	1	ITEM	1,600	1,600

(Note 'R' code signifies a rogue item, not included in cost library)

SANITARY APPLIANCES 5.53 113.76
13,765

Element	Code	Description	Qty	Unit	Rate	Amount
W.C.SUITE	23. 1	W.c. suite in vitreous china, incl. roll holder and grab rail.	30.0	Nr	105.34	3,160
BATHS	2	1700mm long u.p.v.c. acrylic bath incl. grab rails	29.0	Nr	203.93	5,914
SHOWERS	5	Showers incl cubicle, pump, controls and b.w.i.c.	1.0	Nr	328.00	328
LAVATORY BASINS	6	Lavatory basins- vitrified clay; Armitage Shank & "Sandringham"	31.0	Nr	81.41	2,524
SINKS	7	Stainless steel single drainer sinks.	30.0	Nr	61.30	1,839

5.4 Amplified analysis structure — elements to components

achieved. The costs can be sorted so that all the items with the same codes are collated and totalled. Most computerised bill production systems now have this coding and sorting capability. For each component this cost total, divided by the component quantity, will equal the component rate. The component quantities can in most cases be obtained from the bills or from the design drawings. The format used here may be familiar to architects, since it is similar to the analysis costings prepared by ROGER BARBROOK in the *Architects' Journal* under the heading of 'Building Studies'.

Analyses of costs may be arranged in an hierarchial fashion. In figure 5.4 the components are arranged within their element groups so that the sum of the component costs within each group equals the cost of the element. Also, the sum of the quantities of the components within an element group equals the total elemental quantity. Thus, one exercise rather than two provides cost data at both the component and element levels.

The form of analysis shown on figure 5.4 is an amplified analysis. An *amplified analysis* is simply a very detailed version of an elemental cost analysis, as illustrated in figure 4.4. It is important to emphasise that amplified analyses are not revolutionary. They are only a natural progression and refinement of what the QS already does.

This form of analysis may look like a lot of work to create manually, but the reader who is used to using spreadsheet programs will recognise that it is a simple matter to copy the cell relationships from one element and amend to form an other, and to adapt an analysis from one job to serve a successive one. The processing of the analyses uses the Lotus 1-2-3 spreadsheet so that the generation of component costs automatically produces quantities and costs at the 'Element' and 'Group Element' levels simultaneously.

If asked at the feasibility stage, the cost of say a balcony from very little drawn information, the cost planner can at least make a comparative judgement, related to a similar balcony on a previous job for which he might have reliable cost data. However, to try to estimate the cost of such an item from first principles would involve a great number of assumptions, which could be prone to error. Ideally, such items would be defined by sketches at least, but in practice, by the time such items are adequately defined for estimating purposes, it is frequently too late to change them.

One major benefit of this method of analysis using computer systems is that all prices in the bill have to be allocated to components, preliminaries or contingencies. Hence, no costs are missed in the process.

The use of amplified analyses can be further enhanced where the architectural or multi-disciplinary practice uses a reasonably advanced *computer aided design* (CAD) system. Some systems have the ability to hold standard construction details and associated costs and then compute costs according to the areas drawn and quantities generated. The above amplified analysis method of costing lends itself very much to CAD costing methods as these also work along elemental and component lines.

Conclusion

Increasing reliance is being placed upon the accuracy of feasibility costings. Modelling techniques and CAD are increasingly enabling the costing processes to become more refined, accurate and informative. However, a higher quality of cost information is required than has been available using traditional techniques. The method advocated is designed to be more accurate and more informative to clients and design professionals as well as being efficient.

It may be thought by some that we are confusing feasibility work with cost planning. In the computing world generally there has been a strong tendency to form bridges between the coarse, early strategic work and more refined detailed work, which historically has been dealt with only in later stages. What is being advocated in this book mirrors trends elsewhere in feasibility work.

References

[1] NEWTON, S, (1986) 'What is the problem? *Building Cost Modelling and Computers*, ed. PS Brandon, Spon.

[2] University of Reading (1981), 'Cost Planning and Computers,' Department of Construction Management.

[3] SMITH, G *et al.* (1984), *Life Cycle Cost Planning*, Society of Chief Quantity Surveyors in Local Government.

[4] CORNES, RALPH (1986), 'The Smiley's Circus of Unsecret Files,' *The Guardian* 13 November 1986 p 18.

[5] CORNES, RALPH (1987), 'Why Activities belong in Chains,' *The Guardian* 8 November 1987 p 16.

[6] BURBERRY, PETER, (1988), Environment and Services, Mitchell.

[7] Society of Chief Quantity Surveyors in Local Government (1988) *Energy and Cost Planning*.

[8] ELLIS, CHARLES, M & E Computer Spreadsheets, *Chartered Quantity Surveyor*, January 1986 pp 10–11.

[9] WOOD-ROBINSON, M, 'Energy Evangelist,' *Building*, 21 October 1988.

10 WEIGHT, DH, '"Patterns" Cost Modelling', in Brandon, PS, editor, *Building Cost Modelling and Computers*, Spon.

11 National Building Agency Construction Consultants Limited, 'Maintenance Cycles and Life of Building Components and Materials – a guide to data and sources', June 1985.

12 Building Cost Information Service, *Building Maintenance Price Book* 1989.

PART II

six

Costing shapes and spaces

Introduction

In the preceding chapters, the cost models have dealt with broad levels of financial management and the building as a whole. This chapter considers the specific form of the building and the spaces within.

Costing a building as a whole requires making simplified assumptions. Each assumption usually includes an element of error. For example, if it is assumed that space standards per person increase and this in turn increases the building area by, say, 20 per cent, then it may be concluded that construction costs would also rise by 20 per cent. In fact, the cost of a building may rise by less than 20 per cent in many instances. In chapter 4 it was shown that many costs were not simply related to the area of the building but were determined by such factors as the expected number of building users. One reason why costs do not rise directly in proportion to increases in area is that the quantity of many components, such as the number of sanitary appliances, do not necessarily change when the size of a building design is altered.

Need for computer, more than mind can assimilate

Because there are so many variables in design, such as storey height, materials and areas each interacting with the others, computer techniques are particularly helpful in calculating costs and other requirements. Otherwise the design will tend to use rules of thumb such as 'square buildings are cheaper', which in certain circumstances can be misleading. Acting according to rules of thumb may therefore result in abortive work requiring redesign, unnecessarily high building costs, or cutting standards and perhaps areas in order to meet a budget figure.

It is wasteful to revise a design which turns out to be beyond a budget limit, simply because cost information may not have been available at an early enough stage. Developers cannot usually afford a prolongation of design, which delays completion and sales disposal. Often the finance for the purchase of the site is accruing interest, and this loan must be repaid as soon as possible. Moreover, architects cannot afford to do abortive work, for which they receive no extra fees.

According to NEWTON,[1] the step from using cost models for budgeting to using them in the design process has been a difficult one. If cost models do not actually influence the lines that architects draw, the effort spent on feasibility studies remains theoretical; any practical consequences would be lost. It follows that models need to represent and quantify the physical and environmental properties of a building in an informative way.

Communication in the design process requires positive feedback and recognition that messages have been received and understood. When cost modelling is used as a design tool, it should be an interactive process in which assumptions are made and judgements changed jointly. For instance, Thamesdown Borough Council used computer models with architects and quantity surveyors working together to sketch buildings and model the costs. Occasionally, other design consultants joined the team in this process.

Cost models in construction should be developed with the involvement of architects and engineers, otherwise the results of the model may not be meaningful to designers who, without the support of a teamwork approach to costing, often find it difficult to translate their ideas into information which the cost model can use. The cost models allow designers to take greater account of the interdependency of various parts of a building by focusing attention of the inter-relationships that exist, both in terms of construction and use. Moreover, in the absence of a designer's and engineer's input cost, models may often be too inflexible to enable consultants to combine the use of the models with their own judgements.

Computer models

Computer models, such as *Patterns* which is discussed below, have been developed with the involvement of architects and engineers, with consequent advantages over conventional methods. For instance, they use information concerning the technical relationships between the various components and parts of the building. These technical relationships may then be expressed by mathematical rules, which can be inspected and adjusted by the design team. Computer models can easily, quickly and accurately estimate the capital cost involved of heating and lighting a building, taking into account size, shape and the components used. Another advantage of the computer is that the figures presented on screen and print-out can clarify the cost implications of any proposed changes in design and shape.

Interdependence of elements

Relationships between elements are of two types; those elements which are linked physically and those, which are not linked physically but where an indirect relationship exists. Thus, for example, the area of external walls and wall finishes reduces by the same amount as window area increases. At the same time, increasing the proportion of windows to wall area will increase the required capacity, and possibly the size, of the heating plant. New boiler and radiator sizes and associated costs can be calculated automatically by using computers.

Engineering tends to be an aspect of the design in which cost control is particularly difficult. Engineers need to design to cater for the worst foreseeable conditions. Frequently, poor communication in the design team leads engineers to err on the side of safety, over-design projects and incur increased costs. For example, an engineer's initial scheme for an office cooling system may assume normal fluorescent lighting and clear glass. However, the use of high efficiency lighting with high pressure electronic ballasts, coupled with tinted or solar reflective glass, could significantly reduce the cooling load. Cooling is such an expensive item that even if relatively small reductions in the required capacity can be made, significant cost savings are possible.

Role of Computer Aided Design (CAD)

Component costs can be linked to CAD to generate the cost of construction. However, in order for such systems to generate costs, the information has to be defined in detail. Unfortunately, this information is not available at the feasibility stage, when only sketch drawings are made. CAD systems can, nevertheless, supply information on the areas and quantities of building elements at an early stage, though this information still requires interpretation to calculate building costs.[3]

Definition of areas within a building

Areas are usually defined as follows:

Net area is the primary area within which the major activities are performed. In a school, the net area would be the teaching area, including classrooms and the hall; in a block of flats, the area of the flat units only; and in an office, the workplace area.

Circulation areas include foyers, atria, lifts, escalators, stairs, corridors, stairwells and associated landings.

Ancillary areas include all areas which provide communal facilities or in some way support the main activity (or net) areas. These would include toilet areas, or cleaners' rooms. Storage areas may be included in this category, or they may be treated separately. Areas also need to be allocated for plant rooms and ducts.

Gross floor area (GFA) is the area within external walls including stairwells, lift shafts, and atria. The GFA should equal the sum of the net area, circulation and ancillary areas as well as plant room and duct areas plus floor area taken up by internal divisions.

Computer generated shape and quantity

One of the first steps in costing a construction proposal is to ascertain the cost of the outer skin of the building, and consider the relative cost effectiveness of various solutions. The external envelope, which is the sum of the areas of external walls, windows and doors, may be assessed using the following four methods:

1 The external wall ratio is the ratio of external wall, windows and doors to GFA. MOORE[4] has described how the external wall ratio may be used to model and cost a building using data from the Building Cost Information Service. Thus:

$$e = \frac{N}{A} \text{ where } e = \text{external wall ratio}$$
$$N = \text{area of external envelope}$$
$$A = \text{gross floor area}$$
$$\text{Hence, } A \times e = N$$

The floor area multiplied by e gives the area of the external envelope.

This method is, however, unhelpful to most designers and was appropriate only in the pre-computer age.

2 The square index is the perimeter of a building, divided by the perimeter of a square of equal area. Thus:

$$S = \frac{P}{\sqrt{4A}} \text{ where } S = \text{square index}$$
$$P = \text{perimeter}$$

3 The rectangular index is the ratio of the length of a building divided by its average depth. The building depth is the dimension between facing external walls across a building's narrower dimension. If the average span is held constant, when changes are made to the shape of the building, regardless of whether the building is 'T' shaped, 'L' shaped or any other configuration, the rectangular index will remain constant. Thus:

$$R = \frac{P + \sqrt{P^2 - 16A}}{P - \sqrt{P^2 - 16A}}$$

where R = rectangular index

4 The perimeter of a building can be found using the following formula:

$$P = \frac{2A}{w} + 2w \text{ where } w = \text{average building depth}$$

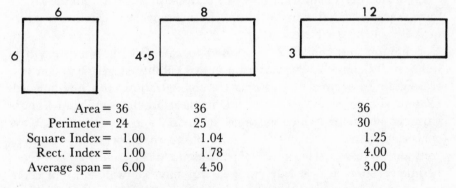

Area = 36	36	36
Perimeter = 24	25	30
Square Index = 1.00	1.04	1.25
Rect. Index = 1.00	1.78	4.00
Average span = 6.00	4.50	3.00

6.1 *Effects of deviations from a square form for similar areas*

All four methods are helpful, especially if they are used in conjunction with each other, for example, using the average building depth to calculate the square index. For most designers, the average building depth is the most informative method of generating the form. The average span between outside walls provides a good early indicator of structural implications, ventilation requirements, as well as many other design factors and their likely costs.

A particular building may have a variety of depths or spans across external walls at various places on the plan. The effect of variation from the average does have the effect of increasing the length of external walls. However, the sensitivity of such variation upon the girth of a building and consequential costs is remarkably low. Usually some extra allowance in computing the perimeter of a building is appropriate to allow for deviation from the average, and to allow for bays, recesses and staggers in the outline.

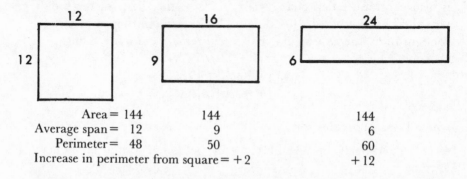

                Area = 144   144   144
      Average span = 12   9   6
         Perimeter = 48   50   60
Increase in perimeter from square = + 2   + 12

6.2 *Effect of variation of building depth upon the perimeter length*

Figure 6.2 demonstrates that, as the plan shape departs from the square form, the same reduction of 3 in the average span produces larger increases in the perimeter.

Computer cost models can be used to calculate the total length of internal divisions. At the inception and feasibility stages of design it is reasonable to assume that alternative configurations of a building will contain similar spaces. Rooms might therefore be shuffled within a variable perimeter which changes in shape and length but always enclosing the same spaces. The sum of the room perimeters remains constant no matter what plan shape is used. An external wall is a room perimeter only on one side, whereas an internal wall forms a room perimeter on both sides. Applying OYLE's LAW of solid geometry, the sum of the length of the inside of the external wall, plus twice the sum of the length of internal walls, including doors, will remain constant, as shown in figure 6.3.

To calculate the total length of internal divisions two methods follow which take account of the relationship of external and internal walls.

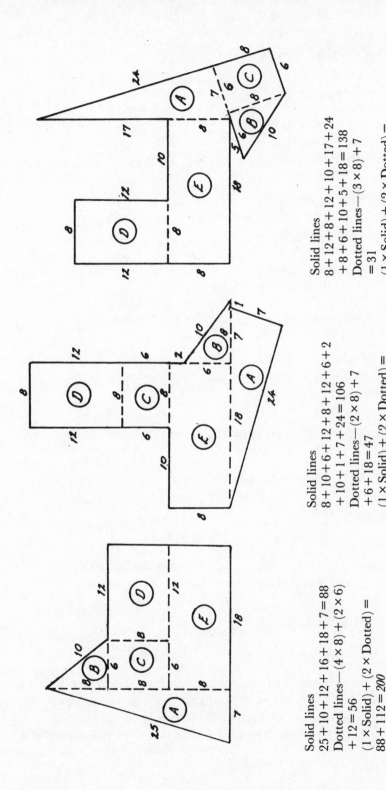

Solid lines
$25 + 10 + 12 + 16 + 18 + 7 = 88$
Dotted lines—$(4 \times 8) + (2 \times 6)$
$+ 12 = 56$
$(1 \times \text{Solid}) + (2 \times \text{Dotted}) =$
$88 + 112 = 200$

Solid lines
$8 + 10 + 6 + 12 + 8 + 12 + 6 + 2$
$+ 10 + 1 + 7 + 24 = 106$
Dotted lines—$(2 \times 8) + 7$
$+ 6 + 18 = 47$
$(1 \times \text{Solid}) + (2 \times \text{Dotted}) =$
$106 + 94 = 200$

Solid lines
$8 + 12 + 8 + 12 + 10 + 17 + 24$
$+ 8 + 6 + 10 + 5 + 18 = 138$
Dotted lines—$(3 \times 8) + 7$
$= 31$
$(1 \times \text{Solid}) + (2 \times \text{Dotted}) =$
$138 + 62 = 200$

6.3 *Spacewrapping*

1 Density of vertical division

Formula: $d = \dfrac{(0.5 \times p) + L}{\text{floor area}}$

where d = density of vertical division
      L = length of partitions
      p = external perimeter

2 Room perimeter method

First, consider a building with square rooms of equal size.
Let N = the number of rooms
    L = the length of a side of one room
    A = the area of each room
and P = the sum of all the perimeters of the rooms.

  (i) $L = \sqrt{A}$
 (ii) $P = 4 \times N \times L$ (since a square's perimeter is 4 equal sides).
(iii) $P = 4 \times N \times \sqrt{A}$
(iv) $\dfrac{GFA}{N} = A$

 (v) $P = 4 \times N \times \sqrt{\dfrac{GFA}{N}}$

Let E = the length of the internal face of the external wall, and
I = length of centre line of internal wall.

(vi) For a given set of spaces $P = E + (2 \times I)$

(vii) $I = \dfrac{4 \times N \times \sqrt{\dfrac{GFA}{N}} - E}{2}$

In order to take account of the fact that the rooms are not all square and of equal size, it is necessary to introduce a factor, K, to account for this.

(viii) $I = \dfrac{4 \times N \times \sqrt{\dfrac{GFA}{N}} \times K - E}{2}$

The above method has an advantage over the internal division method in that the K will usually be more consistent for a given building type than using the ratio of internal division. If the number of rooms is known, and the value of K has been assessed for that building type, then for a given average building depth, the length of internal divisions can be calculated reasonably accurately. The method produces simple statements, which describe the building such as:

'The building is 485 square metres.

It has an average span of 11 metres, making the building about four times as long as it is wide.

It contains 8 large rooms and 5 small rooms.

30 per cent of the external envelope is glazed.'

This clear definition of building form describes the structure and conveys unambiguously the general shape and size of the building compared to using the traditional area and wall to floor ratios. The final quantities should therefore be more accurately predicted.

Services elements

The services elements can also be estimated since these too are determined by the calculated area of various components. By associating U-values (measure of thermal conductivity), and Y-values (measures of thermal inertia), with these components, the areas computed can be used in an energy program to compute the plant requirements and therefore costs. So far the methods used for energy evaluation have been based on CIBS *Energy Guide* Part 2, which is for naturally ventilated buildings. The calculation of energy usage and losses for design conditions have much in common. One model can therefore be used for both functions.

Energy forecasting at an early stage of design tends to be simplistically related to area. However, a high proportion of the energy costs of many buildings are determined largely by the number of occupants, rather than the building's area and its thermal insulation properties. For example, in a school, a high proportion of the running costs will be for cooking and hot water. Ventilation losses, too, should be determined by what people require in order to feel comfortable rather than a predetermined rate of air change based on room areas. This rate would be higher as the number of occupants in a given area increased. After all, it is people who need to breathe, not buildings. Even simple rules of thumb for energy consumption should distinguish between those costs which are determined by the number of building users and those which are determined by area or volume.

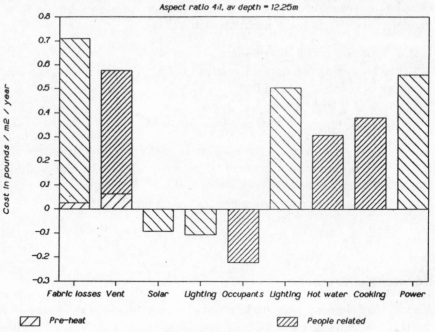

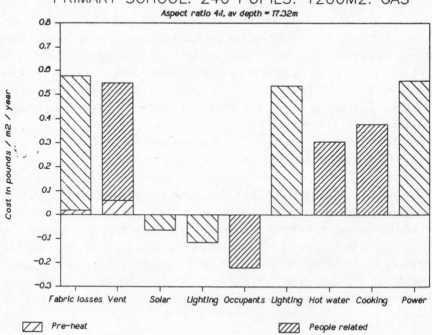

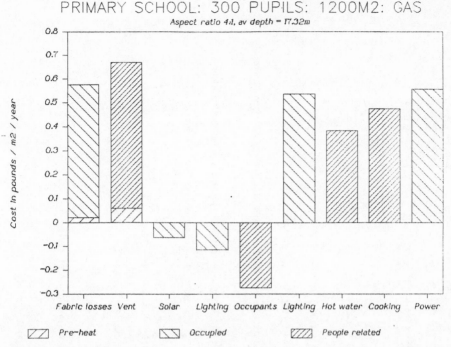

6.4 *Energy consumption profiles for primary schools*

Shape or form

When the plan configuration of a building tends towards the square form, some of the interactions between elements can be described:

1 The length of the external wall and its area will reduce as will the girth of the roof, including eaves, verges or parapets.

2 The length of internal walls and partitions will increase. However, where spaces are arranged in semi-open plan layouts, this relationship will have to be adjusted.

3 As the length of internal division increases then so will the area it covers. Therefore, it will normally have to be of slightly greater GFA in order to contain the same amount of clear space.

4 The proportion of glazing should increase to help maintain daylight levels as more floor area becomes further from external walls.

5 For steeply sloping sites, substructure costs can be reduced by lying a narrower building along the line of the contour. A square configuration would generate more cut and fill and foundation walls as well as resulting in more ramps.

GUIDE TO ASSESSING COSTS FOR SLOPING GROUND (for rectangular areas only)   :> Calculations only
****

(Assumes that slab is all on one level)   Enter

GROUND FLOOR AREA=   400 m2

ENTER > ACTUAL SQUARE INDEX AT GROUND LEVEL =   1.02   (So notional girth=   81.6 m
(Taking courtyards & atriums as if internal area)

Longest side (assumed rectangular)=   24.4 m

RECTANGULAR INDEX (Calculated) =   1.49

Cross-checked girth (now calculated from calculation of sides)=   81.6 m

SO WIDTH (calculated) =   16.38

ENTER > ORIENTATION FACTOR (between 0 & 90, being 0 if parallel)   0   Distance along side nearest right angle to line of contour=   16.4 m
(Equals the angle between longer side and line of ground contour)

ENTER > GRADIENT OF SITE 1 IN -   12   Distance along side nearest parallel to line of contour=   24.4 m

                                            CUT   FILL
ENTER > PROPORTION OF VOLUME OF CUT / FILL   2.00 to 1.00   Height of drop across slope=   1.37 m
(Always answer as if floor is not suspended and rests on exc or fill)

Proportion of depth of cut to depth of fill=   0.59

ENTER > IS THE FLOOR SUSPENDED?   YES   So maximum depth of cut=   0.80 m
(Dispenses with need to fill to u/s of slab)

CUT AND FILL UNDER SLAB:-   and maximum depth of fill=   0.57 m

                        M3   RATE/M3   COST
CUT & C/A   93.68   11.56   1,083   Total M3 of cut=   93.68 m3
                                                Total M3 of fill=   46.84 m3

IMPORTED HARDCORE FILL   0.00   15.50   0

ENTER > EXTRA DEPTH ON AVERAGE, CAUSED BY STEPPING DOWN
          ACROSS CONTOUR, WITHIN FILLED AREA   0.13 m.
          (Each step will usually be 225mm, making average extra depth= 225/2)

          Length of ext wall founds nearer right angles to line of contour=   32.8 m

          EXT WALLS:DEEPER FOUNDS:-   (Meas as length × extra depth:-)

          Length of ext wall across contour which is deepened by fill=   13.57 m

                                    M2 RATE/M2
          ACROSS SLOPE   5.60   62.00   347

          Average increased depth of wall across contour where in fill=   0.41 m.

          ALONG SLOPE   13.81   62.00   856

          Foundation length nearer parallel to line of contour=   48.8 m.

          (At filled end only unless no cut at all)

          Foundation length nearer parallel to contour which is in fill=   24.4 m.
                                    (Above assumes top end is not in fill)

          Increased depth on above foundation=   0.57 m.

OTHER COSTS: (Enter manually)
          To Building: Internal wall foundations   600
                          Slab reinforcement?   0

          Around building: Retaining walls around paths   700
                            Ramps   100

                                                     £   3,686

ENTER > % SUNDRIES & TOLERANCE   5 %

          TOTAL FOR SLOPE OF SITE=   3,870

          WHICH=   9.68 /M2 extra per m2 of ground area.

          6.5 *Modelling the cost effect of slope on site*

Note that the orientation factor may be linked to the energy section as this would affect solar heat gains.

6 Greater depth on plan across external walls means one of two things structurally. If the structural span is across external walls, then these spans will increase in length, and usually in cost terms. Spans over 9 m may be subject to the 1985 Building Regulations on progressive collapse which will add cost. If the span is split, then obviously this necessitates load-bearing walls and/or beams and columns with their supporting foundations. Frequently such walls in rising higher may have to be thickened and strengthened to cater for structural slenderness ratio problems. Generally, the latter form will need a more complex roof structure. It is worth noting that for some buildings, wider spans of floor and roof members can have severe knock-on effects upon crane choice and positioning.

7 The cost of external drainage may be higher for a less square building, since the line of drainage will normally follow round the girth of the bulding and this will be greater.

8 Reduction in external wall should reduce fabric heat losses and therefore the loads for heat source and heat emitters. There should be a small reduction in size and therefore cost of the heat source depending upon sizes available. It may also be possible to reduce the size of the plant room but the relationship between the capacity and cost of the heat source is not directly proportional and in certain circumstances, savings may be slight.

9 Electric lighting will be used for longer periods as a higher proportion of floor area is further from windows. Also the luminaires will have to be replaced more often. This might be mitigated by using rooflights, but these have a cost penalty, as well as losing heat through conduction and radiation. Note that lights may not be high energy users, but their running cost significance may be great, since on-peak electricity is a far more expensive fuel than is normally used for space heating such as gas, coal, or off-peak electricity.

10 Following from points 3 and 5, the mass of the building within the insulated layer will increase, and thus the thermal inertia. A building with a high thermal inertia will take longer to warm up or need a more powerful heat source. Although this can be of benefit to some buildings, for others such as schools, which have very intermittent occupation patterns, it represents an energy loss since there is an increased requirement to pre-heat.

11 As the length of external wall reduces, the scope for spaces with sufficient external walls reduces. Many spaces will require mechanical ventilation and this will increase costs and may add either to the area required for plant, or the storey height to accommodate ducts. The motors for the fans will also need electrical power and maintenance. Ventilation heat loss might actually increase incurring further costs unless strictly controlled.

12 As the depth on plan increases, the build up of heat in the summer, through people, lights, electrical equipment, and solar gains becomes problematic. The effect of opening windows will be less effective for areas near the centre of the building. If such areas rely on natural ventilation they will frequently have insufficient fresh air, may feel stuffy and be prone to overheating. Mechanical cooling is even more expensive per kW than heating, both in initial cost and maintenance cost terms.

13 As the external girth of the building increases, the costs of external drainage may increase as its route follows the perimeter. However, if areas such as toilets or changing rooms have to be sited within the building, this will increase the costs of drainage serving those spaces, as it is cheaper and more acceptable to route drains outside of a building than under it.

14 Square buildings may save on maintenance in that less area is exposed to the weather.

It would therefore be misleading to form a hard and fast conclusion about whether square buildings are cheaper than other shapes. In most instances, particularly tall buildings, it may well be the case. However, for low rise buildings, which require good ventilation and daylighting standards, then a more square building could involve increased costs.

It is often argued that if a building is doubled in size, its shape or plan form may remain similar. Furthermore, a lower proportion of wall area to floor area would result, and therefore the cost per square metre would drop. In practice, if size is doubled, it is the average building depth which is likely to be more constant, and the building form will sprawl more out of square. As a result, the proportion of external wall area to floor area would be the same.

The use of a computer cost model, which co-ordinates initial costs, energy costs and maintenance forecasts will aid consultants to evaluate the knock-on effects of design ideas and decisions at an early stage of design. Its accuracy on many of the above points will not be precise, but it will enable judgements to be expressed. In any case, costs alone will not determine the shape of a building. In keeping with the client's brief, many value judgements must be made.

Concept estimating

A major difficulty in applying cost models to design has been that once an architect has embarked upon a design solution, it is rare for him to seek a radical alternative. One reason is lack of time allowed for design; another is the commitment or attempt to justify design work already carried out. For a cost model to have maximum benefit, it needs to be used before drawings are available, when the project is still a set of ideas. WEIGHT describes two types of computer cost model which have been developed in order to help and encourage designers and clients define their ideas and provide cost information.[6]

Cost model – Patterns

One computer technique used effectively with architects and clients is called the *Patterns method*. This system was inspired by the way that patterns are used for designing clothes. A dressmaker's pattern will show for each size, the amount of material required for, say, a jacket, blouse or skirt. Usually a list of suitable materials is given. The same pattern will hold true for a dress of that shape in any material.

The idea can be applied to buildings, since the elements of a building equate to parts of an outfit. Each design form can be expressed as a kit of elements or parts, and a kit of components can be produced from such a pattern. In fact the patterns are represented by certain key dimensions, such as the average building depth and height, which are then used to calculate the quantities of the building elements. The advantage compared with working from first principles is that when entering the shape data, the architect can relate it to a building with which he is familiar. The shape data is as shown at figure 6.6.

Thamesdown Borough Council set construction budgets and carried out cost planning by manipulating previous building shapes in conjunction with a menu of components. On a community centre project, for instance, a budget was allocated by a committee. A model based upon the

"PATTERNS"

KEY DIMENSIONS *************	Enter for Proposed building	Source model
NUMBER OF OCCUPANTS	300 Nr	300 Nr
GROSS FLOOR AREA=	2,000 m2	2,200 m2
CLEAR HEIGHT=	2.40 m	2.40 m
FLOOR ZONE=	0.45 m	0.40 m

(So storey module=   2.85 m)

CALCULATED QUANTITIES:

PERCENTAGE OF OVERALL FLOOR AREA AT:

Floor areas=

GROUND FLOOR LEVEL	30 %	28 %	600 m2
FIRST FLOOR LEVEL	30 %	28 %	600 m2
SECOND FLOOR LEVEL	25 %	28 %	500 m2
THIRD FLOOR LEVEL	15 %	24 %	300 m2

Check if 100% >   100.00 %

AVERAGE BUILDING DEPTH OR SPAN	15.00 m	14.00 m	1102.00 m2 of ext. envelope
PERCENTAGE GLAZING	20 %	18 %	220.40 m2
NR OF EXTERNAL DOORS	6 Nr	8 Nr	11.70 m2
NUMBER OF ROOMS	20 Nr	24 Nr	
"K" FACTOR OF COMPARTMENTATION	0.97	0.97	333.00 m int. division
INTERNAL DOOR / ROOM RATIO	0.92	0.92	34.96 m2
NUMBER OF STAIRS	12 Nr	12 Nr	
LIFT (assumes to highest level)	YES	YES	
PITCH OF ROOF	30 deg	30 deg	687 m2 of structure,
PERCENTAGE OF ROOF AREA TO BE GLAZED	3.00 %	2.50 %	(measured on flat incl overhangs) So coverings area= 769 m2
THICKNESS OF EXTERNAL WALL	0.28 m	0.28 m	and rooflight area= 24 m2
OVERHANG OF EAVES AND VERGES	0.30 m	0.30 m	(Above assumes no overhanging floors)
PERCENTAGE OF AREA MECHANICALLY VENTILATED	7.00 %	6.00 %	

See judgement areas for services data, such as:
        Ratio of w.c.s and basins to occupants,
        Illumination levels and lumens per luminaire
        Design temperature differences

6.6 *Key size and shape input data*

Patterns principle of a previously built community centre, was used by the architect and cost planner to see what shape, size and quality would be possible within the budget allocation. This helped the architect to proceed with confidence and the exercise minimised the subsequent cost control work of measurement and cost checking.

The steps involved in using the *Patterns method* are as follows:

1   Select the tender and location indices to adjust the cost data in order to bring up to date and account for local market effects on prices.

2   Select the key dimensions of an existing building or design and load into the cost model.

3   Adjust the shape and size of the source model to reflect the required building.

4   Select the components the proposed building.

5   Review the component rates used, particularly where the rate will be affected by the building shape, such as roof structure, or ventilation.

6   Verify heating plant capacity requirements with engineer.

One difficulty of this method is that some source models have to be prepared. However, where a cost analysis consists of one building, then most of the shape information that the model requires can be calculated from the areas of elements. For instance, the average span and square index can be computed from the height of the building plus areas of external walls, windows and external doors. This is simply putting the modelling formulae into reverse. The analysis program uses actual areas to work out dimensions and the model uses dimensions such as average building depth, to calculate the quantities of components required.

Cost model – Spacewrapping

The Patterns approach may be impractical if a reasonably similar building cannot be identified and analysed. On very large complex buildings, it may also be difficult to visualise the model from verbal and cost statements. A different approach is to cost model the building's requirements as they develop during the design process.

The function of a building is to wrap up spaces. WEIGHT (1987) describes a new type of cost model called *Spacewrapping*, which has been developed to help define the client brief in such a way that it can be costed at an early stage and be of use to designers.[5] Spacewrapping can be described as an inside out approach to design.

At the very earliest stage, the information concerning a client's requirements only consists of the functions of certain areas, a broad statement of the quality required, and usually the overall size. Drawings are unlikely to be prepared at this stage. Spacewrapping is designed to make explicit the implications of the brief in terms of cost and the quantities of components even before drawings are prepared. It therefore requires a well co-ordinated approach from the design team, particularly with regard to the structural and environmental services elements.

Zones

The Spacewrapping approach deals with the building on a zone by zone basis. A zone can be defined as one room or a collection of rooms. Where one zone contains more than one room, such rooms usually perform similar functions, and will be of similar quality with regard to finishes, heating and lighting standards. This corresponds to current good practice on briefing, since rooms within one zone tend to be dealt with collectively.

An architect will carry out an initial exercise on the building to assess the best relationship between spaces by drawing sketches of alternatives. Planning, fit on site and aesthetic considerations must of course be taken into account. The zones used in Spacewrapping tend to correspond to the spaces an architect will show in his early sketches.

Once a shopping list of components has been selected and costed, the procedure for using the Spacewrapping program can vary but includes the following distinct steps:

1 Ascertain the net areas the client requires. This may be assessed from area analyses of similar building types with which the client is familiar.

2 Estimate the areas which will be required for ancillary purposes, including, for example, toilet areas, storage areas, and communal facilities such as a lounge, shared kitchen, and reception area.

3 Estimate the proportion of the building used as circulation spaces by comparing area analyses of similar building types. Circulation spaces include corridors, atria, staircases, lifts and escalators.

4 Estimate the area of the building required for plant and vertical ducts.

Then, using the computer:

5 Enter the average area of, and number of each functional zone. In Spacewrapping, not only is the data set in hierarchial form (components within elements), but so are the spaces. The area data is entered for each functional zone. The area at each storey level is the sum of the zones at that level. The total building area is the sum of the areas of each storey level. If computer power and memory allows, one could work at the level of each room, but this would be very unwieldy and time consuming.

6 Use the rectangular index to express the shape of each zone, which generates the girth of each zone. (This will advise the average width.) Figure 6.7 shows an extract of the model showing the input for steps 5 and 6.

7 Enter the shape parameters for each storey level. Determining the average span is probably the best method. (This average span informs both the rectangular index and the square index and calculates the length of external wall.)

8 Estimate the proportion of external windows and doors, expressed as a percentage of the vertical external envelope.

9 Select the tender and location indices to adjust the cost data to bring it up to date and account for local market effects on prices.

10 Choose components which occur throughout the building, mainly the external and structural elements, such as roof, frame, external walls, windows, and external doors.

11 Enter the specification selections for each zone, eg finishes, internal doors, lighting, etc. Figure 6.8 shows an extract of the model showing the input for this step.

12 Carry out sensitivity analysis to see which factors have the greatest influence on cost, by, for instance, altering assumptions concerning foundation depths, specification quality or plan depth. The two most difficult elements to anticipate are probably structure and ventilation. For most of the other elements, quantities and costs can be generated with confidence, provided that cost data is of good quality and judgements concerning market and location factors are cautious.

13 Use the facility of trying alternatives to optimise the design in conjunction with the brief, costs and planning requirements. When carrying out this step, the information entered in the preceding steps can be revised in any sequence.

```
EXTRACT OF "SPACEWRAPPING": ZONE DATA
******************************************

            ZONE 4:-  PAIRS OF CLASSBASES
            COST/ZONE=      57,038 COST/M2=      485.01
            FLOOR AREA PER ONE ZONE=           115.20 m2
            *************************************************.
                                                 Enter:
    SIZE    CLEAR FLOOR AREA FOR ONE ZONE=       115.20 m2
*********(Incl own store,and allows for rising 5s).

            NO OF THIS ZONE=                      5.5 Nr

    PLAN    RECTANGULAR INDEX=                    1.80

    SHAPE   so perimeter =            44.80 m
**********so length=       14.40 m
            and width=        8.00 m

EXT.WALL? EXTERNAL WALL REQUIRED ?               YES
*********
            (External perimeter assessed by apportioning
            of zone girths)=         19.30 m

            NR. OF EXTERNAL DOORS =                2 Nr

 INT.WALL INT. WALL TO ZONE PERIMETER (Total perim.
********** - girth on ext.wall)=     25.50 m

            NR OF INT. DOORS BORDERING ZONE=       1 Nr

  ROOMS    LENGTH INT DIVISION WITHIN ZONE=    13.10 m
  WITHIN
  ZONES    NR. OF DOORS SERVING COMPARTMENTS WITHIN
**********ZONES (Excl. w.c. cubicles)=           2 Nr

 SERVICES NUMBER OF POWER POINTS                 8 Nr
**********
            ILLUMINATION LEVEL (LUX)             340

            UTILISATION FACTOR FOR LIGHT=        0.45

            AIR CHANGES/HR WHERE MECHANICAL=       0
```

6.7 *Extract of Spacewrapping*

AQ70: (,2) (AO70*AP70/100)   READY

	I	J	T		AO	AP	AQ	AR
1	10	10	8	1	10	12	10	10
2				2	ZONE 4:- PAIRS OF CLASSBASES			
3				3	COST/ZONE=	57,038	COST/M2=	485.01
4				4	FLOOR AREA PER ONE ZONE=			115.20
5				55				
56			Unit	56	Potential	Enter	Selected	Costs for
57	Specification choice		Rate	57	Quantity	Choice %	Quantity	for one zone
58	===========================		=58	==			
59	Hardwood block floor		37.00	59	115.20		0.00	0
60	Vinyl sheet (Poly f		25.40	60	115.20	40	46.08	1,274
61	Rawson magnum 3000"		21.00	61	115.20	60	69.12	1,528
62	Higher quality carpe		26.60	62	115.20		0.00	0
63	Quarry floor tiles o		45.60	63	115.20		0.00	0
64	Mondo profile studde		0.00	64	115.20		0.00	0
65	Coir yarn mat in gal		130.00	65	115.20		0.00	0
66	"Junkers" Beach floo		46.00	66	115.20		0.00	0
67	Maple floor		0.00	67	115.20		0.00	0
68	Carpet at doorways w		28.00	68	115.20		0.00	0
69				69				
70	95 * 19 s.w.skirting		3.87	70	64.50	100	64.50	250

24-Apr-89 06:57 PM   CALC

6.8 *Extract of Spacewrapping*

Following this procedure, Spacewrapping enables the cost breakdown to be viewed both in elemental and component form. The locations of these cost can also be clearly ascertained as a design develops.

Using computer cost modelling for refurbishment work

The estimation of refurbishment work is always more difficult than for new build work. A cost modelling technique which may be of use when information is limited involves the following steps:

1 Model the size and shape as if the refurbishment were new build.

2 Deduct or reduce the costs of all elements, which are unaffected or only partially altered by the proposed refurbishment work. Typically, these elements will be substructure, external walls and roof.

3 Increase the rates for all elements the cost of which is greater because of obstructions.

Caution must be exercised, as there are great difficulties in costing refurbishment work. The state of the existing building may pose problems, which cannot be easily foreseen prior to a detailed survey and design. Nevertheless, as long as these difficulties are understood, then the technique described may be applied as a helpful guide.

Costs will be higher than for new build for various reasons. Productivity will tend to be relatively low because of disruption and poor, often cramped working conditions. The diverse activities and treatments required mean less repetition of work. The rates for many services elements will be high because of the difficulty of incorporating them into a structure, which was not designed to accommodate them. Examples of services include electrical wiring, communications and pipework. On-site supervision and office overhead costs will also tend to be high. Finally, there is less opportunity for bulk ordering of materials and obtaining discounts and at the same time material wastage will tend to be high.

Enlarging the financial cost model

The feasibility study can be made even more useful to the client if the effects of predicted costs and revenues can be shown in a broader financial context. This overview will usually include land costs, fees, building costs and sales values. The cost and timings of these items are usually worked out separately. Computers enable all these factors to be incorporated and modelled together. This permits each factor to be varied and changed in conjunction with others. For example, the advantages of a faster but more expensive form of construction may be looked at in terms of earlier revenue income, reduced interest payments and faster turnover.

Time

The time factor is important, and this is especially so on projects which have letting or sale contracts agreed subject to completion dates. Certain factors will increase the pressure for faster design and construction periods. One reason may be to avoid high finance charges, which increase with rates of interest and duration of the project. Even in the public sector, on a large prestigious project such as a leisure centre, there may be a great political will to meet advertised times and pre-opening publicity. Many private sector clients require that money committed to one project is returned and reinvested as quickly as possible, to achieve a fast growth rate. Public companies who are quoted on the Stock Exchange, usually take this view.

The principal factors which influence the duration of a normal project are:

1 *Size of project*, which is best measured in terms of its area.

2 *The form and method of construction.*

3 *Ground conditions.*

4 *Time of year for starting on site* Consider in conjunction with points 2 and 3.

5 *The site* Where the area around a building is tortuous and restricted for circulation and storage, this puts more pressure on the building for this purpose, making working conditions more cramped. Also plant such as forklift trucks cannot be used as efficiently.

6 *Height and number of storeys* A six storey building will take longer to build than a three storey building of the same area (other things being equal). This is because work progresses in layers or storeys and more men can work on each larger storey level with less interference.

7 *Wet trades* such as plastering and screeding will take longer to carry out, and time will have to be allowed for curing.

8 *The method of procurement* and the selection and skills of the project management, design team, and the contractor.

Following the receipt of tender and the contractor's programme of work, it is theoretically possible to calculate an expenditure profile, showing the costs of the various stages of work. However, this exercise is time consuming and expensive and the programme itself is usually subject to alteration. In any case, at the feasibility stage, this information will not be available. It is therefore reasonable to base the expenditure profile in the feasibility study on historical trends for similar types of jobs, but amended according to the list of factors above.

Ideally, the items used in the valuation should relate to stages of work referred to in the contractor's programme of work. This approach enables easier reconciliation with the contract programme when this is produced, and helps to provide early warning if a project is not progressing on time.

The valuation should be plotted graphically. The graph depicts the cashflow trend in terms of the proportion complete each month. The resultant graph of the whole project tends to be the shape of a lazy 'S' (see figure 6.9). For this reason, a series of such curves are usually referred to as *S-curves*.

TREND FOR 29 MONTHS

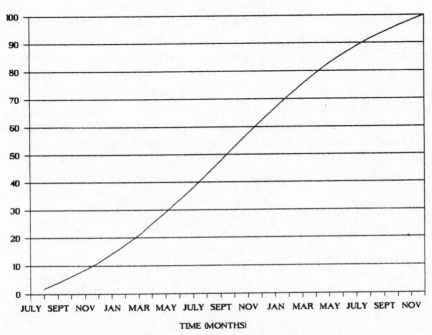

6.9 *Typical lazy S curve depicting construction expenditure profile*

For some clients, not only is the overall cashflow and project viability important, but it may be necessary to have a forecast which predicts the financial position in any one accounting period of even the time of year. It is, of course, possible to take seasonal factors into account. The construction cost expenditure curve is based upon the contract sum, the contract period, the averge cost trend (or S curve) for the type of job, and the productivity factor for each month. The productivity factors account for the fact that output per man will be lower in poor weather, the effect of holidays at Christmas, Easter and August, and the fact that the average working day will be shorter in the winter months.

Average trends of previous years can be applied to sales or disposal of buildings. This might seem problematic, but feasibilities often have to be carried out very quickly, and an approximation based on an established seasonal trend is quicker to assume than to try to assess each factor individually from first principles.

Having calculated the above items, as illustrated in figures 6.10 and 6.11, these can be consolidated to compute interest costs, overall profits and percentage return on capital expended.

Such a program can test the effect of a whole range of variables in a few seconds. This might include interest rates, construction periods and various land costs to establish the likely variances and risks. Notice that the construction expenditure curve in figure 6.12 is now shown as negative, in order to distinguish it from revenue, which is shown as positive.

Some clients and companies base their figures on current costs and current values, whilst others attempt to forecast at outturn costs and values. When current costs are used, it is assumed that revenue inflation trends will at least compensate for any increase in the building tender

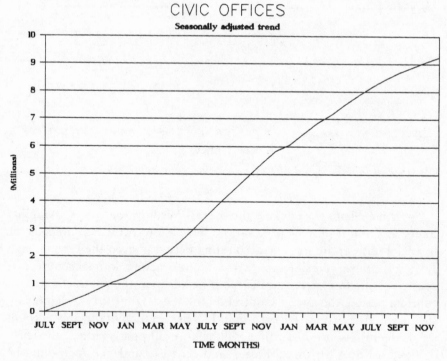

6.10 *Seasonally adjusted S curve*

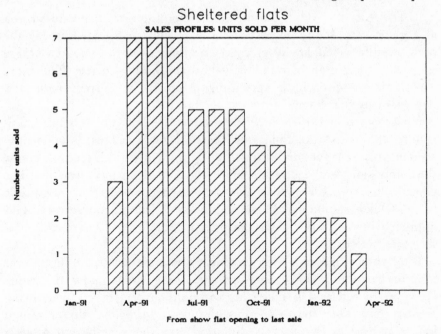

6.11 *Sales trends*

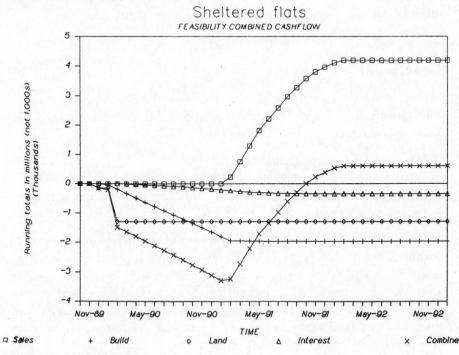

6.12 *Composite cashflow*

cost. The reason for this is that it is too difficult to rely upon values rising at a given rate. Many property developers incurred great losses in the mid-'seventies when, having enjoyed a few boom years they invested large sums in anticipation of building values continuing to rise. The more conservative approach of appraising a project at current costs and revenues can guard against this.

However, to ignore revenue inflation altogether can miss important factors. If the effect of time and interest rates upon cost is taken into account, but revenues are assumed to be static, then this tends to create the impression that delays are more costly than in fact they are. The effects of inflation on revenues may be looked upon merely as a possible bonus, which should not be relied upon for feasibility purposes. This approach obviously increases the pressure for shorter design and construction periods.

If inflation is ignored, projects tend to be more profitable the shorter the construction period, assuming everything else remains the same. However, if inflation is taken into account, expected revenues, being greater than costs, may rise more than costs, provided that revenues inflate at least as fast as costs. Inflation may therefore benefit projects with longer construction periods, though this increased profit is often offset by an increased exposure to risk and uncertainty.

Conclusion

A design cost model must help to answer the questions an architect may ask. Design is a process of making choices. At the simplest level, for building construction, these choices are:

What size and shape should be drawn?
What components should be used to form these shapes?
What should be the environmental quality (principally, light and heat) and, how should it be achieved?

The methods described above should enable costs to be forecast to within a reasonable range of accuracy on most projects, provided the design team can define the approximate building form, space and quality standards. This means that a client brief can be developed and refined before the client has made a major financial commitment or embarked upon any specific design solution. This speed and accuracy is greater than was possible before the introduction of the new computer hardware and software standards in the 1980s.

Computer cost modelling brings great spin-off advantages with it. For instance, each design consultant can learn more about the technology of the other disciplines in the team. Another advantage is that modelling simulates experience. The ability to explore alternatives quickly, builds up an understanding of which variables are the critical factors. The benefit of an increase in knowledge gleaned from participating in one scheme may be applied to future projects.

References

[1] NEWTON, S, (1987), 'What is the Problem?' in Brandon, PS, editor, *Building Cost Modelling and Computers*, Spon.
[2] SMART, DA, (1987), The importance of CAD/BQ link for the 1980s.
[3] ATKIN, B, (1986), 'Making experience count', *Chartered Quantity Surveyor* May 1986 p 15. 'Time for CAD', *Chartered Quantity Surveyor* July 1986 p 13.
[4] MOORE, P, (1988), 'Working along the right lines', *Chartered Quantity Surveyor* October 1988.
[5] SEELEY, I, *Building Economics* (1983), The Macmillan Press Ltd.
[6] WEIGHT, DH, (1987), ' "Patterns" Cost Modelling', *Building Cost Modelling and Computers*, ed PS Brandon, Spon.

seven

The brief and cost control

Introduction

The need to communicate a client's requirements to his design team is met by the *brief*. It is a document which ideally will have emerged after a process of consultation and negotiation. However, there is no formal procedure for arriving at the brief and the usefulness of the final document depends very much on the personalities of those involved in its writing and execution. Nevertheless, the briefing process is closely linked to the study of feasibility, as advice on the brief should be based on a systematic appraisal of costs and requirements, whether the building is to be used for owner occupation or rented.

Setting the brief priorities and objectives

The first step in the development of the client brief is to define the objectives or the needs which are to be met. It must be established if the project is purely profit motivated, such as a speculative private housing estate, or whether the project's purpose is for social benefits, such as a National Health Service hospital. Some projects may have a political value which cannot easily be evaluated, such as the Channel Tunnel. In practice, many projects will have to satisfy more than one of the above aims. From the objectives come the needs and the functions to be performed.

Before appropriate quantity and quality standards can be ascertained, some market research is necessary to help assess the scale and viability of the project. The existing and future demand and social or market values need to be ascertained. When projects are for sale or rent, valuers or letting agents should be consulted. For many projects, a study of historical trends such as shown in figure 7.1, may assist in such assessing future demand.

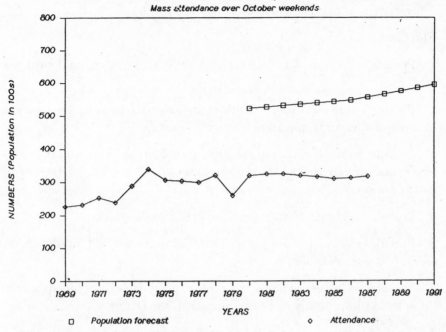

ST AUGUSTINE'S PARISH, ST AUSTELL
Mass attendance over October weekends

7.1 *Numbers of attendance at a church*

Having specified the functions which the completed project must fulfil, these need to be quantified. Initially the units will be expressed in terms of the likely maximum number of users, or the units of utility. For example, in a school project it will be the number of pupils; for a marina, the number of boats; and for a road bridge it will be the maximum number of vehicles per hour. Multi-purpose buildings should be broken down according to their functional areas. Thus a shopping arcade might include car-parking, public toilets and restaurants.

A *client brief* is a statement of the uses of various areas of a building. It will normally cover space standards and quality or performance standards for the various zones as well as the building as a whole. It should also set out certain requirements for many of the external works elements.

The building is not the aim but the means by which a client's objectives may be achieved. The areas for each space can only be ascertained in the light of judgements relating to needs. These needs are the objectives of the building and each requirement or objective should state a function, a quantity (usually an anticipated number of people likely to use the space), and a statement indicating the quality of the space. An example of such a set of objectives might appear as follows:

III

Chinese Cultural and Trade Consulate Centre[1]

Objectives of the development in order of priority.

The Centre aims to:

1 Provide education facilities for 100 children at infant and primary levels.

2 Provide leisure and sports facilities for 120 adults similar in standard to those at the Pineapple Dance Studio, London.

3 Provide library facilities to accommodate 50 readers plus an information centre similar in standard to the main library at the Polytechnic of North London.

4 Provide children's library facilities for 15 to 20 children.

5 Provide personnel offices for up to 10 full time staff and public offices, serving 20 visitors at any one time.

6 Provide a Chinese artifact and consumer goods exhibition space for up to 200 visitors at any one time, similar to the Design Centre, London.

7 Provide meeting facilities for up to 40 business people for commercial and trade meetings.

8 Provide work display space for a maximum of 6 small firms similar to House of Fraser department stores.

9 Provide one cookery classroom with professional catering facilities for up to 20 students in any one class.

10 Provide caretaker accommodation with two double bedroom flats.

For the client, there are at least four main areas of concern. These are *quantity*, *quality*, *cost* and *time*. Anticipated value, sales revenue or rent are not usually targeted in the same way since they are outside the direct control of decision makers. However, the four factors above are usually considered critical to the success of a project. In the brief, targets will often be set. Thus, cost limits or budgets will be given, the size and requirements of a project indicated, standards specified and the date for completion stated. This chapter deals with each of these critical factors in turn and shows their implications for the effective control of projects.

All relevant assumptions and judgements must be made explicit. If certain elements of a building are left vague the architect may assume one thing, the QS another and the letting agent yet another. It is therefore vital that all consultants involved make consistent assumptions about the building at all stages of design. The next step is to determine the areas required to serve the required functions.

Establishing user requirements for the brief

In order to establish a schedule of areas and therefore total space requirements, it is often necessary to carry out a user requirement study. The study is usually broken down into smaller studies of groups of areas, or zones. These groupings will usually correspond to areas of management responsibility, once the building is occupied. Where an existing organisation is planning to use the new building, its various managers should be consulted about the requirements of their areas of responsibility. For instance, the zones in a leisure centre might be: ice rink and associated areas; swimming pool, including wet changing areas; gymnasium, weight training and keep fit areas; and central administration. These groupings should be broken down still further. Again, where possible, more information may be required from individuals, who either plan to work in the rooms within these groupings or are specialists in their particular field. For example, a specialist area such as weight training will call for an understanding of the type and size of equipment needed, the circulation area required and the clearance between activity areas to ensure the environment is safe. It must be admitted that the management process of evolving the client brief through consultation with staff and maintaining an harmonious working environment is a difficult, sensitive and delicate exercise. Extreme tact and diplomacy are called for.

It is sometimes necessary to define the precise dimension of a space, such as a squash court. Often it is necessary to state the area and approximate shape of a particular room, such as a toilet for disabled persons. However, for the major part of most buildings, it is sufficient to state the overall area requirement of a collection of rooms, grouped according to their function. This is usually sufficient for administration areas. This approach is speedy and straightforward to define, and gives the architect scope to design.

Analysing areas for the brief

One difficulty in agreeing a schedule of areas is defining the sizes and dimensions of spaces in a formal manner. It can be most helpful in

```
BUDGET MODEL AREAS
--------------------------

NAME -     PRIMARY SCHOOL
----------------------------------------
DESCRIPTION -          330 PLACES
----------------------------------------


--------------------------------------------------------------------------------
1  TEACHING            Classrooms         11 bases at   55.00 m2   :        605
                       Audio visual room                          :         40
                       Hall                                       :        130
                       Balance                                    :         43
================================================================================
TEACHING AREA, Same basis as D.E.S.Regs                           :        818
(Including associated internal division,but excluding storage).   :
--------------------------------------------------------------------------------
2  TEACHING STORAGE    Classroom Storage  12 No. at     3.00 m2   :         36
                       PE Store                                   :         10
--------------------------------------------------------------------------------
3  PUPILS CLOAKROOMS   Coats Storage      11 bases at   2.00 m2   :         22
   AND CHANGING ETC.   Pupils toilets                             :         43
                       Changing                                   :         12
--------------------------------------------------------------------------------
4  ADMINISTRATION      Head                                       :         12
                       Secretary                                  :         14
                       Deputy Head/Group/MI                       :         15
                       Staff room                                 :         25
                       Staff toilets                              :         10
                       Stock rooms                                :         18
                       Caretakers base                            :          5
                       Caretakers Store                           :         12
                       Cleaners Room                              :          3
                       Staff showers                              :          3
--------------------------------------------------------------------------------
5  ANCILLARY           Kitchen                                    :         45
                       Chair store                                :         24
                       Boiler House                               :         15
================================================================================
NET AREA                                                          :    - 1,142
--------------------------------------------------------------------------------
BALANCE    (circulation)                                          :
     Total of areas 1 to 5 at              17.0 %                 :        194
================================================================================
GROSS FLOOR AREA                                                  :      1,336
================================================================================
```

7.2 *Analysis of areas*

discussions between the client and his advisers, if they all know the areas of rooms within familiar buildings. They can then make adjustments from one or two such benchmarks. Figure 7.2 shows a typical area analysis upon which judgements about space requirements might be based in the light of a user requirement study.

Moreover, areas of completed schemes may not always be measured in a way which enables reconciliation with an original brief, with the result that subsequent design briefs may be misconceived. This method of area analysis can therefore be very useful for clients who build frequently.

Shape, or configuration is also difficult for many clients to describe accurately. Fortunately, it is sufficient if clients describe rooms or spaces using plain language such as, 'about square', 'twice as long as it is wide'. A rectangular index can then be used to respond to these statements, which will compute the zone perimeters and average widths within seconds. Slight misjudgements in assessing this index are very rarely cost significant. The Spacewrapping computer program (described in chapter 6), was designed to assist this process and avoid abortive work.

Discrepancies between the areas defined in the brief and those actually built can arise for a variety of reasons. The area as briefed may be cut to satisfy budget constraints. When succeeding buildings are proposed, it should therefore not be assumed that a previous building was indeed the size as briefed. The brief is often regarded by the client as flexible and can be changed as the design develops. The architect may also see the brief as being flexible and adapt it to suit the shape of his design. When this occurs, tight budgetary control and reporting of cost effects is difficult. If not identified early in design, the final analysis will not correspond to predictions and expectations.

Specifying standards for the brief

The study of user requirements should also include references to quality and performance standards. For example, the requirement for floor finishings and partitions in a wet changing room may state that the surface must be impermeable and non-slip yet easy to clean and washdown, with partitions clear of the floor for this purpose. Specific finishes or components should not be defined at this stage.

Environmental standards should be indicated by stating average levels of illumination and temperature differences capable of being maintained between inside and outside temperatures. Indicative criteria should also be set out for ventilation and cooling where appropriate.

A user requirement study is rarely incorporated into a client brief without adjustment. What the building's users want and what they get are two different things, since the client can rarely afford to satisfy the needs of all potential users. The final client brief will evolve through consultation with managers, department heads or tenants depending on circumstances.

A compromise solution will usually have to be found and often it is up to the architect, acting as the expert adviser to resolve, in negotiation with the client, the problems of competing requirements and contradictory objectives. The architect will also have to take into account many other factors. These may fall outside the scope of the client brief, depending on the shape of the design and statutory requirements, such as the provision of fire escapes and toilet areas. There are also many occasions when a combination of onerous planning requirements and a tight or awkward site, make it impossible to design closely in accordance with the client's brief.

Developers may expect their architects to achieve various standards and targets which all appear reasonable when looked at independently of each other, but when looked upon as a whole package may be contradictory. For instance, a client may stipulate good quality air conditioning, a high number of storeys and a high net to gross floor ratio. Unfortunately, a high number of storeys will generate greater vertical circulation and the high quality air conditioning will possibly use a large plant room as well as area for ducts. These areas will be in addition to the lettable or net floor area and will increase the gross floor area, reducing the net to GFA ratio. By modelling the interaction of various factors using computers, assumptions can be rectified and objectives modified.

Adaptability

Determining space standards can be very difficult if the occupancy or use of a building is likely to change. This is a common difficulty when assessing the accommodation needs of a company, which is either expanding or changing its working methods. Flexibility is important, and by allowing a few design margins in the brief, adaptation of the building is possible. Indeed, it is essential to consider alternative uses for many building projects in order to provide the building with an after use. This will substantially reduce the risk associated with a project, since the disposal value of the building in the worst possible scenario will be to some extent protected.

Designing to meet minimum current standards and minimise initial costs can effectively restrict the client's future options, for example, by preventing extensions on the site without having to buy more land. Future improvements may generate excessive costs, and adequate upgrading may even be impossible.

Many office buildings built in London to minimum requirements and storey heights in the 1960s were unable to adapt to incorporate the air handling and cabling requirements of the computer hardware of the 1980s. If the floor to floor storey height module is designed to a minimum, with little or no provision for mechanical air treatment, it will effectively rule out the possibility of refurbishing to a higher quality at a later date. As a result it has often proved cheaper to demolish and rebuild many offices in London than refurbish them.

These factors are not always considered by clients when they set tight cost limits for a development, and there is always a danger that better long term economy is sacrificed in order to meet short term budget constraints. If a short term reason is put forward for saving money, to counter it often requires an extremely robust, clear and well documented argument, of the type advocated in this book. Fortunately, the principles of life cycle costing are increasingly appreciated. Indeed, it is to spread that word, that this book has been written.

Costing and pricing a proposal for the brief

The general viability of a scheme can be gauged by using rough data, including a sketch design from an architect from which measurements can be taken. Early costing of construction work is often based on an estimate of the cost per square metre of GFA. An analysis of the areas of previous buildings of a similar type will provide an indication of a likely net to gross floor ratio. The gross development or capitalised value can be calculated from the net floor area, the rental value per square metre (or square foot), and the expected percentage annual yield. The residual valuation method for valuing land described in chapter 4 can then be used to examine the cost, revenue and profit implications.

We have shown how cost information may be combined with cost models to provide accurate costings. However, this alone is not sufficient. Increased accuracy is of no benefit if the assumptions about the needs, use and size made by different members of the construction team are inconsistent with each other.

If the final cost of a project is far in excess of its original estimate, it has been argued, then feasibility studies have little validity and relevance. However, it is vital that the original assumptions in a feasibility study are understood by the design team. If the design team are to design within budget, then the design has to be subject to cost control. This does not mean that the design should be in a financial straightjacket. As plans proceed, circumstances change and clients may alter their instructions. New decisions have to be taken almost on a daily basis. Any modification has to be seen as improving or detracting from the existing plan. Any change has to be considered in financial terms either saving or increasing costs. The designers therefore need to evolve their design with an understanding of what they are evolving from! The starting point is the feasibility study.

On large buildings, design responsibility is often delegated to various architects for large areas. Responsibilities can become blurred. Cost discipline may be hard to maintain as each architect tends to design as he wishes, in the hope that the work of the other architects will not in total overshoot the budget. However, the Spacewrapping approach may be used to monitor and control the costs of each component and element in each function zone. Thus, for cost control purposes the building may be treated as a collection of buildings, each with its own cost plan.

If different areas are to be funded in different ways, then spacewrapping can help with the allocation of finance and design for each area. If tenders are based upon a bill of quantities, then by giving each area a location code in the taking-off process, the prices in the bill may be collated according to these codes. The brief and feasibility study are therefore critical in setting up the project and managing it effectively.

Conclusion

The development of the client brief is itself a process of great importance to the success of a project. It is vital that the contents of the brief are communicated to the design team and understood and interpreted by them. The process consists of the following activities:

1   Establishing and defining the needs of a proposed building's users.

2   Balancing these objectives with various constraining factors to produce the client brief, which is then a full statement of requirements.

3   Establishing that cost and revenue forecasts are satisfactory. Identifying the critical factors and refining requirements in the light of these

findings. Indeed if a project is deemed not to be feasible then it may be abandoned before further time, effort and money is expended on further investigation and design.

4 Ensuring that the final product and its cost is related to the feasibility study. Control, monitoring and agreement of all changes can be carried out on the basis of the brief, not only during the design and construction phases but also throughout the building's useful life.

One of the main purposes of a feasibility study is to discuss the client's brief in more detail, relating the objectives the client may have with any specific requirements as well as the constraints of the situation, such as shortage of suitable land at a reasonable price, and planning requirements. No computer can know what is in the minds of a particular local planning authority, which in most cases will not have participated in the cost modelling exercise.

References

[1] CHIN, PHILLIP HF, post graduate Dip Arch student, extract from thesis report, Polytechnic of North London 1989.

eight

Feasibility studies and the client

Introduction

Whatever type of client and his motivation, there can be little justification for embarking on large projects without first systematically carrying out a feasibility study of the options.

The experienced client will, or should, know what he wants. This is probably the paramount requirement in the whole costing process. Indeed it is· the major reason for expensive redesigns and budget overspends. The experienced client is unlikely to disrupt the design process. The client's statement of space and quality requirements is known as the *client brief* and was discussed in more detail in chapter 7. The final brief should be written in the light of a feasibility study.

The experienced client should know how to assemble a team and delegate responsibility. In a large client organisation, the distance between those who hold responsibility for funding, and those involved with the project, tends to increase. This may be physical distance or a distancing caused by the internal politics of an organisation. Very often it is difficult to find out exactly who the client is. In large public bodies, relationships between departments and between the levels of responsibility within departments are often strained, complicated and arbitrary. It is understandable that those with responsibility for spending will not always agree with those who hold responsibility for design.

Even where a corporate client plans to be the owner-occupier, there are often tensions between those who represent the building users and those who authorise financing as well as the usual inter-departmental rivalries. A compromise building solution, which satisfies everybody is frequently impossible. These tensions nearly always have financial implications.

Those people in higher levels of authority will rarely have time to listen to the detailed problems of design or construction. However, summarised cost forecast figures tend to have a more immediate impact. If the individual responsible for funding has a choice between a cheaper shorter term solution, and a more expensive higher quality building, it is usually opportune for him to opt for the former. This may not always be in the long term interests of the organisation. The likelihood of long term maintenance problems and user dissatisfaction with a building will not necessarily be of primary importance to the decision maker, who may well have moved on or up from his current position in the firm by the time these problems become apparent. However, a large budget overspend will often reflect badly on an individual's career prospects. To ensure that long term considerations are in fact taken into account, while at the same time avoiding a budget overspend, it is essential for a feasibility study to be conducted.

Developers and the feasibility study

A recent article in the *Sunday Times*, discussing the approach of one particular developer, summarised his five basic steps to property development as: 'Find the right site, tie it up, get planning permission, find tenants and find finance'.[1] In order to minimise the risk of not achieving the objectives at each stage, it is essential for the developer to devise a strategy based on a feasibility study.

A feasibility study will provide the developer with a timetable and cash flow, taking into account possible difficulties and the likelihood of delays, which will help to assess the risk involved. Applying the same systematic approach to each proposition, the developer can compare different options with a view to selecting the proposals, which increase the firm's asset base the most, by choosing the most profitable projects.

The developer's profits are his motivation for taking the risk that either the selling price of the building or rents will be insufficient to cover costs. Maximising these profits is usually assumed to be the prime motive of the developer. However, it is rarely the only motive. Although much property is owned by individuals, it must not be forgotten that a society is composed of its individual members and increasing their assets increases the total wealth in a community. The question remains as to whether or not the distribution of these resources reflects the political preferences of the society.

Nevertheless, from a developer's point of view, a building is like any other form of investment. He will seek reassurance from the feasibility study on the following points: he will require a clear indication of likely revenues allowing for growth; the building should be a hedge against inflation; the building should be economic to operate; the building should be easy to sell at any point in its expected life, either to a new occupier or as an investment proposition to another property company.

Finally, the tax position of the developer may affect his decision regarding the feasibility of an option. The taxes of most direct concern to him will be corporation tax and capital gains tax. Value added tax (VAT) and income tax also affect the position and cash flow of developers. If a building is a secure investment with the possibility of capital appreciation, perhaps because of future developments in a locality, the rate of return required on the initial investment will tend to reflect the lower risks. Hence in general, the lower the risk, the lower is the yield.

A project that is feasible from one point of view may not necessarily be viable from another. The developer's point of view will be different from that of others in the locality of the site. As these points of view will usually be in conflict with each other, there is no one solution to the problem of feasibility. In spite of the understandable temptation on the part of the developer to maintain secrecy concerning his plans, it will always be necessary for the interested parties to negotiate and compromise. Giving too much information away will enable sellers to raise prices charged to a developer; objectors will be able to organise themselves, causing delays and raising costs out of proportion to their objections (from the developer's point of view); and rival developers may be able to compete for the site and so drive up prices and reduce profit margins still further.

The feasibility of a project depends on the requirements of the developer, who will need to be assured of the existence of an effective demand for the building or the services provided by its occupants. The broad interests of third parties directly affected by the proposals and the perspective of pressure groups such as preservation or conservation groups will often also have a bearing on the feasibility of a proposed scheme.

Each party in a dispute may choose to commission a feasibility study of its own. Each will have its own set of priorities. Often, however, individuals or groups opposed to schemes will be less organised and less able to afford the costs of expert advice. However, to the author of a feasibility study, different clients will want to emphasise different priorities and want to obtain different information and answer different questions. This highlights both the limitations and the usefulness of feasibility studies as decision tools. No one feasibility study can satisfy all the demands of all the parties to an issue but it can focus the discussion on the points at issue.

As noted in chapter 7, it is essential to establish the needs of the client before embarking on an involved document which fails to satisfy the client's requirements and answer his specific questions. In the private sector, developer clients may be intending to use the building for their own use, they may be developing a site for sale, lease or rent; they may even be interested in appraising a given project in the first instance only for the purpose of comparing it with other completely different alternative projects they may have identified.

In the public sector, government departments, local authorities and public corporations will often be concerned with political and social objectives as well as the usual issues of cost. As every situation is unique, it is not possible to lay down a model feasibility study which would be useful in all cases. Each study has to be tailor-made to fit the client, his needs and the size of the project.

Nevertheless it is worthwhile to note the type of analysis that may be used by developers to establish the profitability of a project. It is clear that the client's main priority has to be to avoid losses, minimising risk in order to maximise profits. To do this the client will often take a narrow financial point of view and disregard those costs of a project that will be borne by others but for which there is no legal obligation to pay compensation. At the same time the client's financial interest would not be affected by any benefits to a local community for which he received no payment. These factors do not come into his strict financial reckoning as they do not directly affect his cash flow or help him to repay his loan from a bank, financing institution or other source.

In preparing feasibility studies it is useful to distinguish between clients in the private and public sectors as illustrated in figure 8.1. The private sector can be further divided into profit motivated developers and non-governmental organisations which may be non-profit orientated, such as charities wishing to develop a site to provide a service. Pressure groups, like *Greenpeace*, may also be involved in the planning process and therefore require a feasibility study to articulate and highlight the problems posed by changes to the environment.

Private sector feasibility studies for profit motivated clients

This section deals with feasibility studies directed at the questions raised by clients, whose main concern is to develop sites profitably. It is the duty of advisers to advise. If problems are anticipated it is the duty of the professional consultant, writing a feasibility study to prepare the client. In this way difficulties may be overcome or at the very least allowed for in the budget. Indeed the problems may be of such an intractable nature

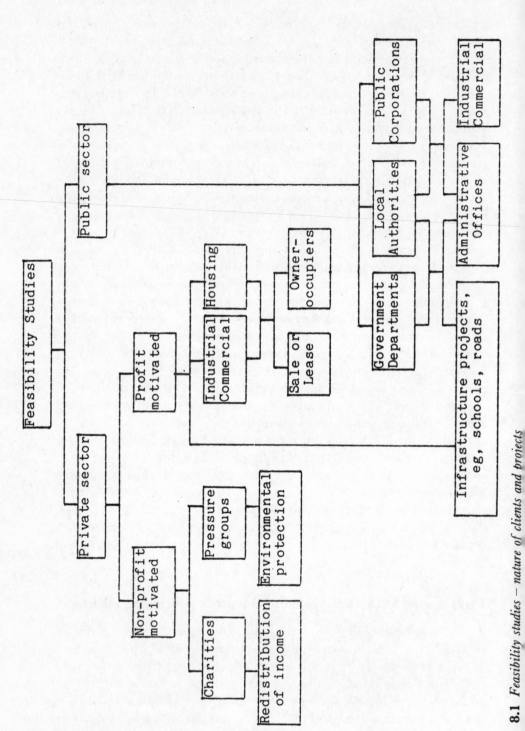

8.1 *Feasibility studies – nature of clients and projects*

that it may be in the client's interest to halt a development altogether. Such advice at an early stage may enable funds to be diverted. Even though a project may be aborted as a result of a feasibility study, just as in any scientific pursuit, the rejection of non-viable proposals is an essential part of a systematic approach. In medicine, for instance, spending time and money to research a possible cure only to discover that the treatment is ineffective, is useful if only because it illiminates possibilities and narrows the choice. Similarly, to establish that a project is not worth undertaking may be as important and useful as justifying one which should go ahead.

Often a developer's early calculations are designed to find the upper limits of a possible bid for a particular site based on a residual land valuation. As shown in chapter 4, land value is the residual after the costs of construction, professional fees, cost of finance and developer's profits have been deducted from the likely income from the sale or lease of a given building.

It is of course possible to change any of the assumptions used to derive cost figures, including rates of interest, the duration of the construction contract and the market value of a completed building. Each scenario can be investigated and the results may highlight possible critical factors. Each assumption should be clearly stated so that changes can be inserted into the same model for the purpose of making a comparison.

More detailed cost calculations would still be needed to establish budgets and tenders which would be consistent with an original cost plan. The advantage of the Patterns and Spacewrapping systems described in this book as well as other computer programs linked to CAD is that they make it possible to maintain a flexible design strategy as cost implications can be re-assessed quickly and reliably as the design progresses. This can be achieved by using computer techniques and programs.

INCOME	£	£	£
23 3-apartment flats @ £36,000	828,000		
34 2-apartment flats @ £29,000	986,000		
13 1-apartment flats @ £24,000	312,000		
		2,126,000	2,126,000

COSTS			
Cost of land	250,000		
Cost of construction	1,000,000		
(£900,000 + £100,000 bonus)			
Architect's fees	100,000		
QS fees	40,000		Continued ...

Insurance	10,000	
Contingencies	100,000	
Marketing costs	50,000	
	1,550,000	1,550,000

Cost of borrowing on tap @ 15% p.a	139,125	
(Assumes sales completed in month 18)		
TOTAL COST INCLUDING INTEREST		1,689,125
PROFIT		436,875
Add grant		70,000
Total profit		506,875

Note: The schedule shows the assumptions made in the possible phasing of the loan.

	Schedule of finance on tap	
Month	Amount borrowed £	Total £
1	100,000	100,000
6	150,000	250,000
9	250,000	500,000
12	500,000	1,000,000
15	500,000	1,500,000

In chapter 3, discounted cash flow tables showed various options, each with a value on disposal. For instance, Table 3.1 showed a development costing £8 million with an expected disposal value of £16 million and an annual net income of £1.6 million. In other words, as a rule of thumb, it would take approximately ten years to purchase the property out of annual net income. The multiple, in this case, of 10 is called the years purchase and is the inverse of the required rate of return to the developer after tax and interest payments. In the example in chapter 3, 10 per cent was chosen as the target rate of return, reflecting a relatively high assessment of risk. This values the building pessimistically. An optimistic or low risk assessment would justify the acceptance of a lower rate of return to investors, who would hope to make up for the lower rate of return by making a capital gain on disposal of the assets. A very low rate of return might be around 3 to 5 per cent. A rate of return of 5 per cent would produce a years purchase of 20 and a value of the same building of

£32m, (20 × £1.6m). The value of a building depends on the years purchase, which in turn depends on a subjective assessment of risk.

Several factors have to be considered when calculating the net annual income. The rent or imputed rent is based on lettable floor area, which may be only 70 to 80 per cent of the GFA, since up to 30 per cent of a building may be taken up with circulation space and services. It is usual for rent reviews increasing rent, to take place every three to five years on industrial and retail premises. Rents on office premises may be reviewed every 5, 7, 14 or even 21 years. The net annual income is the gross rental income less the landlord's expenses including fees to land and letting agents.

Thus one of the main advantages of conducting a comprehensive feasibility study is that it enables the client to refine the brief, by eliminating the contradictions and specifying the project in quantitative terms and setting targets for future managers to achieve. Managers operating in the completed building may set target figures for sales, staff accommodation, building use, occupancy rates and so on, based on the assumptions contained in the feasibility study.

Feasibility studies for non-profit making organisations in the private sector

Non-profit making bodies, such as charities, may have difficulties in assessing sales revenues, especially if the service provided is free to users. Consequently, its objectives may be to provide the maximum quantity of its product or service to the maximum number of people at the highest quality possible and as efficiently as possible, that is with the least possible waste. Thus, efficiency involves employing the minimum resources necessary to achieve a given aim. However, it may be perfectly possible to provide a service efficiently, even though that service or product may not be needed. Nevertheless, setting such objectives does not necessarily require a knowledge of revenues, only costs. The difference between managing a project efficiently and maximising profits is that efficiency considers costs alone, whereas profits take both costs and revenues into account.

Profits are the difference between total revenues and total costs. Costs measure the value of resources used to produce a given output, which can be a service or a product. When cost per unit of output is at a minimum, an organisation may be said to be efficient in terms of the resources it uses. Although an organisation may be a non-profit making institution, it will nevertheless have every incentive to be efficient. No charity, for instance, could allow itself to be described as inefficient. Indeed, running a charity efficiently in terms of the return on its capital is much the same as profit maximising behaviour.

For profit orientated firms, consumers' demand is reflected in sales revenues. If a non-profit motivated organisation assesses demand, even indirectly, by imputing values on its service, it will enable managers to plan and set targets. Indirect methods of assessing demand are dealt with in chapter 11.

Ranking options in non-financial terms

In looking at alternative objectives, non-financial priorities, such as the number of users of a charity and the quality of the service it provides, need to be examined. One method of comparing each proposal's merits is to use a points weighting system, which allocates points to each of several objectives. Each proposal is then given a percentage score against each objective depending on how well the option is expected to fulfil a particular requirement. These percentages are then multiplied by the respective weighting to produce a total number of points. The totals of each option can then be compared to find the one which provides the greatest overall benefit in terms of the stated alternatives.

How the points are allocated to each desired objective to produce an order of priorities is contentious, since consensus may not be possible. Either an average is taken from a number of responses to a questionnaire or expert opinion may be sought. Whichever method is used, the resulting weights are likely to displease significant numbers of those interested in a given project. One reason for this is that different individuals or groups of individuals will have their own interests at heart. Objectives which favour some may harm the interests of others and this approach does not in itself resolve these difficulties. Moreover, assessing the potential of a given proposal to meet certain requirements is very much a matter of judgement.

Until a building project is finished and in use, there can be no firm assurance that the results will be as predicted. However, it is possible to introduce confidence limits and ranges, for instance, by stating the probability that an option will achieve between say 60 and 70 per cent of a given objective. The end result will require interpretation and the ranges of totals for each option may well overlap with others.

Because of these difficulties, feasibility studies often ignore the problem of assessing benefits by assuming they are the same regardless of the option chosen. If any factor is identical for every option, it can safely be ignored, since the purpose of any comparison is to highlight significant differences between proposals and not their similarities.

If benefits are ignored, the problem then becomes one of finding the least cost solution for a given physical proposal. This method is known as cost effectiveness and has been dealt with in chapter 3. Where an organisation is not only concerned with financial costs, non-financial costs should also be taken into account. A charity, for example, may rely heavily on volunteer helpers and an estimate of the value of their time should be included in order to assess the alternative uses to which their labour could be directed.

Feasibility studies for clients in the public sector

Similar problems arise in the public sector to those confronting non-governmental non-profit making bodies. The Treasury, however, has directed that public sector projects should be handled in a similar way to profit making organisations. Public sector projects have to generate acceptable rates of return on capital invested. Yet government often directs its departments of state to undertake projects which have little or no hope of achieving a commercial rate of return. Such projects are often carried out for political reasons and are not the subject of systematic analysis but rather the cut and thrust and compromise of the political system. Nevertheless, it is still possible for economic solutions to be worked out in detail, with the aim that the political objectives are met in deed and in spirit, with the minimum possible waste of resources.

The question arises which target rate of discount should be applied to projects in the public sector. The minimum rate of discount used by the Treasury is currently 5 per cent. Public sector projects which generate a positive NPV at this rate are therefore acceptable to the Treasury on this criterion, other criteria notwithstanding. This rate of discount for public sector projects is not very different from the real after tax rate of discount, which was 4.6 per cent in the 1980s for projects with an average level of risk based on after-tax rates of return.

Feasibility studies therefore in the public sector are no different from those in the private sector, except that many of the costs and benefits will be in non-market goods, making it necessary to assess the values using indirect methods, such as questionnaires and surveys. It should be noted that, even in the private sector where goods are traded, there may be market imperfections making it necessary to carry out similar exercises. Indirect methods are also needed to value consumer surplus, which is the difference between the amount people would be willing to pay and the price actually paid. To estimate the real value of a benefit, the value of consumer surplus should be added to expected sales revenues. Thus, if a product or service is free to users, such as the service provided by general practitioners under the National Health Service, then its entire value is the value of the consumer surplus.

References

[1] DAVID, G, 'Eddie builds a shoppers' dream,' *The Sunday Times*, 7 August 1988 p D5.

nine

Feasibility studies and the architect

Aspects of the legal framework

Architects have a legal obligation to provide their clients with reliable cost information, even when there is no written contract between an architect and his client. Though the major and minor works editions of the *Architect's Appointment* replaced the *Conditions of Appointment* in July 1982, contract documents may incorporate the relevant edition of the *Architect's Appointment*. Clause 2.25 in the major works edition of the *Architect's Appointment* requires the architect to 'carry out cost planning for a building project, including the cost of associated design services, site development, landscaping, furniture and equipment; advise on cash flow requirements for design cost, construction cost and cost in use'. As KINGS points out: 'In fact, one must assume that every architect is in a position to offer the advice on costs required of him. In any event the client is entitled to receive such service at a professional level and indeed, it is hard to imagine how the architect can survive without a fairly detailed knowledge of costing.'[1]

Litigation may result if, for example, buildings exceed an agreed budget. It is not a question of suing the architect for the difference between the expected figures and the actual cost. The issue arises, when payment to the architect is withheld, following a budget overrun or if tender prices are unexpectedly excessive and the proposed building is not started. Architects may not only forfeit their fees, but also find themselves liable for their client's legal costs. In legal terms, an inability to provide the client with effective cost information may lead to 'a failure of the consideration' made for the services of the architect. A 'consideration' is the payment made under the terms of a contract and the legal phrase implies that the practice has, to use KINGS' phrase, 'not kept its part of the bargain'.

Although many architects may prefer to avoid lengthy discussions about costs, BUGG offers practical advice for practices including knowing how to present costs and being confident of being in control, knowing what is happening, what is likely to happen and demonstrating this confidence to the client.[2] This advice spells a knowledge and understanding of the techniques and applications involved in writing feasibility studies, which architects now require.

Feasibility studies and the design process

As noted in previous chapters, discussions at the feasibility study stage will be concerned with the broad design and the expected overall budget throughout the anticipated life of a building. It is possible and desirable to alter details of the design and demonstrate the impact on costs, present values and rates of return as well as the possible extension or contraction of the period of construction. Such exercises demonstrate the sensitivity of the project to certain changes or variations in the planned scenario.

In fact the feasibility study will enable the architect to get the most out of the resources available. In this respect the architect may be able to realise design opportunities, which might otherwise have been abandoned as intuitively impracticable. Alternatively, the architect's own time can be saved by not pursuing design ideas, which would prove too expensive to construct. It is therefore important for the architect to receive sound cost advice not only from a quantity surveyor but also from structural and services engineers.

To establish the cost of a building project for pricing purposes, it is necessary to examine the design proposal under five broad headings. These are:

1 Function
2 Quantity
3 Quality
4 Planning requirements
5 Abnormals

Various aspects of a building's function are dealt with in chapter 7.

Quantity

To provide the QS with the information he requires to generate the building cost, drawings should, of course, be drawn accurately, so that areas can be scaled. If the scale is drawn as markings along a ruled line, then shrinking or stretching caused by copying or faxing can be accounted for. If a computer model such as the Patterns system (described in chapter 6) is used, it is possible to assess the quantities by referring to previous buildings of a similar type.

Quality

Specification standards for all parts inside the proposed building should be clearly stated. If items such as balconies or lifts and escalators are required, information specifying performance, capacity and special finishes should be included.

Planning requirements

In order to check for compliance with planning permission, both plan and elevation sketches or drawings are needed. An indication of any complicated structural work is also useful at this stage. The architect may have to specify particular material, such as natural stone walling or natural slates to comply with a planning requirement.

Abnormals

Any features of the site which will have a bearing on costs should be included with the above information. Certain abnormal features will directly affect the building, such as the slope of the site, demolition both above and below ground and the quality of the ground itself, especially if it is soft and requires piles. If piling is necessary, the length of piles should be stated. Other abnormal features of a site will concern the external works or services, including drainage of surface and foul water, overhead cables and diverting existing sewers. Information may be required concerning tree preservation orders, retaining walls, walls shared with neighbouring premises, and other work in connection with adjoining property.

Thus, various factors with significant cost implications are relevant to the architect during the design process, including: the plan shape, which produces a perimeter to floor area ratio; the size and planning of the building; storey height and total height of the building; the column spacings and floor loadings; the quality, ease of manufacture and expected useful life of materials and finishes; the length of the construction period; the repetition of building components and elements, that enable early commissioning of the building. Finally, an allowance for unexpected cost increases is needed to protect projects from going over budget. Such contingencies are necessary because of design changes and complications which usually arise in the course of construction including delays caused by weather conditions, late deliveries of materials and labour disputes.

Growth in importance for architects of studying feasibility

Since the de-regulation of the architectural profession, the importance of feasibility studies for architects has increased at an accelerating rate. Competition for work has increased both in foreign markets and from abroad, in the UK market. This increased competition has led to a need for professionalism in the marketing of design services. No longer is personal contact sufficient to secure contracts. A display of professional competence is required from the outset in establishing a working relationship with potential clients.

Traditionally the architect has been an 'artist, designer, planner, builder, fixer, technician, problem solver'. Though he should not lose sight of his traditional role, O'NEILL argues, an architect is or should also be able to act as an 'entrepreneur, opportunist, enabler, developer, fund raiser, code changer, marketing man, management man'.[3] He sees the modern architect capable of being a professional businessman and asserts that, 'The dynamic relationship between architectural values and the needs of commerce – not always a happy one – creates livelier debate today than ever before, and is everywhere producing better buildings'.[4] Whether or not one agrees with O'NEILL's assertion, most commentators would agree that lively debate and improved architecture form desirable objectives for systematic analyses of building proposals.

The architect's marketing tool

The feasibility study is the marketing tool of the designer. It enables the architect to introduce specific projects or proposals, demonstrating an understanding of different aspects of a scheme and an ability to handle the complex financial and managerial problems involved before, during and after the construction phase. The feasibility study is the device which architects can use to communicate with other professionals and clients from the earliest stages onwards. After receiving a brief from a client, a feasibility study will often constitute the most appropriate response from the architect. In it he can show the client how he has taken the brief on board in the design. At this stage it is still possible to negotiate with clients to justify a particular design decision or to alter the design to accommodate the client's latest wishes. To that extent the feasibility study documents may be used as a negotiating tool.

However, the feasibility study may also be used by the architect as his sales document. It is the report he can present to a potential client to demonstrate his understanding of the design in terms the client will require, namely the financial requirements.

This is also important for the architect developer who needs to seek finance on his own account. He needs to demonstrate his professionalism by approaching his financial backers with a competent financial presentation. At the least the feasibility report will enable him to feel confident during the meeting which will raise his chances of achieving the desired outcome.

Aid to planning

Feasibility studies have many other uses for the architect. It enables the architect to plan. CHARLES THOMSON of ROCK TOWNSEND described the planning process relating to the Middlesex Polytechnic building at Bounds Green in North London, stating: 'We needed to develop a strategy for a phased development of the project over the following decade and we needed to get the first phase onto site as quickly as possible'.[5]

Firstly, there is a need to plan the building in terms of its local environment. At this stage the architect is very much concerned with land use and planning permission. An early visit to the planning department of the local authority with sketch drawings, even before embarking on the feasibility study, will often greatly assist in establishing the potential massing, storey height, number of dwellings or other restrictive covenants on the site. Later the study can be useful in planning applications and enquiries. For this reason it has to be a balanced document anticipating objections and difficulties and suggesting possible solutions.

Secondly, feasibility studies imply a need to plan within the architect's own office. The number of professionals, their quality and the hours of design time required are all indicated by the size and timing of the project. After all a building is only feasible if it is possible to fit it into the office schedule of the architect or his sub-contractor.

Feasibility studies as part of the service offered by architects

Because of the very specialism of architects it is often appropriate for them to conduct feasibility studies on behalf of clients, who may be seeking solutions with design, flair and imagination. Increasingly architects and designers and indeed others involved in the construction industry are required to produce feasibility studies for clients, without necessarily then going on to create the buildings proposed. A given site may be sold with planning permission, obtained with the help of a feasibility study.

Having conducted the feasibility study of a proposal, another firm of architects may be awarded the commission to design the actual building. This may occur for several reasons. The client may have an existing working relationship with another practice, or he may wish to keep a management team together. The firm which carries out a feasibility study may not be able to deliver the design service in time to meet the client's needs. Finally, a practice which prepares the feasibility study may not be large enough or have the experience and track record, specialist expertise or reputation required for the project.

As a result of current trends in this field, it is likely that in future architects and their consultants will undertake far more feasibility studies for projects, which they are then not asked to build. The ability to prepare feasibility studies for clients will be seen as just one service amongst others which architects and designers offer. For designers the design concept will play a central role, since the design itself must be acceptable on aesthetic grounds but the feasibility study will go on to illustrate the social, political and economic context of a proposed design. Only then can it be determined whether or not a particular proposal is financially and economically sound.

In a sense, the architect must wear two hats, when developing a feasibility study. His two roles may at times be in conflict with each other. On the one hand it is important for the architect to take the widest possible view of his work, taking into account all those who may be either beneficially or adversely affected by the project to find the optimum solution for the problem posed in the original brief. At the same time the architect will have to carry out the instructions of his client, demonstrating that he has financial and economic competence to handle the sums of money involved and manage the construction and running of the building. The design is not seen as separate from these other activities since the good design must be economic to construct and efficient to run. The designer may be seen as an integral member of the organisation team, which operates during the period of construction as well as throughout the expected life of a building.

The construction period

An understanding by the architect of the problems of construction management will help the designer of the building to anticipate some of the site problems and reduce the costs of construction without in any way detracting from the quality or size of the project. On the contrary, good management will enhance the possibilities of making improvements during construction rather than constraining the design.

Most building projects follow a similar pattern of cash flow, often referred to as the S curve, as discussed in chapter 6. To begin with the financial commitment to a building project may be minimal, only increasing when the site is purchased. As the construction period commences expenditure begins to rise and continues to rise at an accelerating rate as more men and materials are brought onto the site. As the building nears completion the rate of increase in funding declines as machinery is removed from the site and labour is no longer required in the numbers needed during the main construction phase.

Although the building cost will be the cumulative total of all expenditure on the building up to completion, it can be understood from the S curve that not all of the funding is required from the outset. By carefully phasing the construction of the building and only drawing on funds as and when invoices from the building contractors and consultants become due, considerable savings can be made by the architect on behalf of his client. The S curve can also be used to monitor progress during construction and hence help to control costs, anticipate problems and delays and co-ordinate activities on site.

By working to establish the S curve, the whole construction management team, including architects, quantity surveyors, services engineers, building contractors, sub-contractors and site managers will be able to appreciate their own contributions and timing in terms of the overall effort to erect the building. The S curve may be derived from the network

NETWORKING   Enter start date of first activity   02-Jan-89
JOB: Ferndown   Enter date of progress report if job is current   15-Jan-89
                                  Date of this print   31-Jan-89

Showing dependency of row activities upon column activities.

1	2	3	4	5	6	7	8	9	13	14	15	16	17	18	Activity number	Activity Description
															1	Setting out / Site set up.
0.4															2	Foundations excavate and concrete.
0.8	0.5														3	Brickwork to d.p.c.
1.0	0.8	0.2													4	Drainage
	1.0	0.6	0.4												5	Precast floor to ground level
		0.8		0.3											6	Brick and block to u/s of first floor
					0.2										7	Scaffolding erection
		1.0		1.0	0.7	0.2									8	Structural steel to u/s first floor
					0.7	0.2									9	Precast floor to first lev & p.c. sta
				1.0		0.5	0.4								13	Brickwork to u/s plate
							1.0	0.5							14	Roof carcassing
						1.0		0.8	0.3						15	Brick / blockwork to u/s roof
								1.0	0.4	0.2					16	Flat roof
								1.0	0.4	0.2					17	Felt batten and roof tiling
	1.0							1.0				0.6			18	Rainwater goods

NOTE: Figures less than 1.00 may be entered above if dependent activity can commence before preceding activity is complete.
E.g. If brickwork can commence when concrete foundations are only 40% complete, enter 0.4.

9.1 *Time management network*

of activities of the various participants in the building process. The whole construction process is broken down into individual activities and their expected duration. Some activities will require to be carried out consecutively while others will be done simultaneously (or in parallel) with others. By knowing the likely duration of each activity, the earliest possible date of commencement of any one activity can be planned. Clearly, by finding the date of completion of the last activity, the date of completion can be established. By carrying out as many activities in parallel as possible, the period of construction can be reduced considerably.

Critical path analysis (CPA) may be used to find a path of consecutive activities through the maze of all activities. Each activity on the critical path is important in that the whole project will only be completed on time if every activity on the critical path is completed within its allotted time. Activities which are not on the critical path may have slack associated with their duration to the extent that a slight overrun will not necessarily affect the final completion date.

Figure 9.1 shows a relatively basic and simple, but nevertheless useful

Activity duration	Enter actual %-age done at report date	Earliest Start	Earliest Finish	Latest Start	Latest Finish	Float	Denotes if critical	%-age planned to be done at report date	Earliest Start	Earliest Finish	Latest Start	Latest Finish
5	50	0	4	0	5	0	Critical	37	02-Jan-89	01-Feb-89	02-Jan-89	06-Feb-89
4		2	6	2	6	0	Critical	3	14-Jan-89	11-Feb-89	14-Jan-89	11-Feb-89
5		4	9	6	11	2		0	28-Jan-89	04-Mar-89	10-Feb-89	17-Mar-89
5		5	10	18	23	13		0	04-Feb-89	11-Mar-89	09-May-89	13-Jun-89
3		7	10	8	11	2		0	18-Feb-89	11-Mar-89	02-Mar-89	23-Mar-89
6		8	14	8	14	0	Critical	0	25-Feb-89	08-Apr-89	25-Feb-89	08-Apr-89
19		9	28	10	29	1		0	03-Mar-89	14-Jul-89	10-Mar-89	21-Jul-89
2		12	14	16	18	4		0	26-Mar-89	09-Apr-89	24-Apr-89	08-May-89
3		12	15	13	16	1		0	26-Mar-89	16-Apr-89	05-Apr-89	26-Apr-89
6		14	20	14	20	0	Critical	0	08-Apr-89	20-May-89	08-Apr-89	20-May-89
7		17	24	19	26	2		0	28-Apr-89	16-Jun-89	12-May-89	30-Jun-89
5		19	24	24	29	5		0	14-May-89	18-Jun-89	18-Jun-89	23-Jul-89
2		20	22	27	29	7		0	21-May-89	03-Jun-89	09-Jul-89	23-Jul-89
8		20	28	21	29	1		0	20-May-89	15-Jul-89	28-May-89	23-Jul-89
4		25	29	25	29	0	Critical	0	25-Jun-89	23-Jul-89	25-Jun-89	23-Jul-89

Time to completion= 29

29

time management networking system, using a computer spreadsheet program. The steps involved in its use are as follows:

1 Define each activity.

2 Type a brief description in the column provided proceeding down from one row to the next in approximate chronological order.

3 Enter the duration for each activity.

4 Execute an automatic mechanism which forms a split screen effect (known as *windows*), and puts the cursor to the left of the topmost activity description.

5 Where the timing of an activity shown in a row depends upon an activity whose number is shown in the column, enter numbers between 0 and 1 in the matrix provided. An entry of 0.5 will indicate that the dependent activity (row) may commence as early as half-way through the duration of the activity shown in the column.

6 Use the appropriate function key to calculate the worksheet.

Once a job is under way, the percentage showing progress made may be entered for each activity. Where no entry against progress is made against an activity it is assumed that its rate of progress is as planned.

A term currently in use in the construction industry is *fast track*, which is simply the application of CPA, with a view to cutting the period of construction to an absolute minimum. This may involve hiring extra labour at specific points during the construction phase. Close working relations with suppliers are encouraged so that materials are delivered punctually, even to the hour, to minimise storage, the risk of damage, handling times and costs. The equivalent approach in manufacturing industry is known as *Just in Time* (JIT), which reduces the need, risk and cost of holding stock. Fast track also involves the whole management team in frequent meetings. The architect is in an ideal position to orchestrate and motivate the management team to meet the requirements of fast tracking.

The feasibility study will include assumptions about the cost and duration of the construction period. Clearly, as the costs of construction occur in the initial period of the life of a building, these costs have a significant weighting in the discounting calculations. If some analysis of the construction costs can be carried out at the feasibility stage, then the question of how the building is to be constructed will have been considered.

The building in operation

Of course the life of the building only commences on completion of construction and to ensure that good management practice is followed through to the operation of the building, the designers must plan the building accordingly and inform the final building users how best to take advantage of the building's design features and organisation. Extracts from a project's feasibility study would make communications with final building users and managers consistent with the original concept of the building design.

The various uses of the building will have been specified in the feasibility study. Moreover, the design will have incorporated many features arising out of the client's brief. A full description of the size and type of activities associated with the internal spaces of the building would have formed the basis of calculations to establish the value of the building. Traffic flows, numbers of building users and the variety of activities will determine the quality of the building, the quantity of services required and the construction systems adopted. If these are to be appropriate they must be consistent with the actual use of the building spaces.

Spaces within the building may be viewed by the design team, for the purpose of the feasibility study, to be either profit centres or cost centres. As the name suggests, some activities will provide a service for which income will be forthcoming, either in the form of rent or sales revenues. Other parts of the building may be seen as necessary but incapable of generating revenues in their own right: examples of cost centres include atria and circulation spaces, which require cleaning and maintenance, toilet and cloakroom facilities, which require the services of attendants and landscaping which requires constant upkeep. Cost centres are often necessary either as an integral part of a building's function, such as cloakroom facilities in a cinema, or in order to increase the revenues of the profit centres, such as retail outlets, by providing extra amenities to attract individuals into a shopping centre. Car parking spaces may be profit centres in some buildings while in others, some of the spaces provided are a cost, where they are provided free to the user.

Conclusion

For the architect, feasibility studies are useful for negotiating the terms of the brief with the client, providing a set of instructions to the occupants for the efficient management and maintenance of the building. They also form an effective and professional marketing tool for architectural practices as well as comprising one of the many services they may offer.

References

[1] KINGS, J, 'Legal Obligations', *Architects' Journal*, 10 August 1983 p 63.
[2] BUGG, V, 'Current Practice', *Architects' Journal*, 3 August 1983 p 44.
[3] O'NEILL, DC, C THOMSON, D ROCK and A HAY, *Architects and their work, Transactions*, Vol 5, No 2, RIBA 1987 p 53.
[4] ibid p 54.
[5] ibid p 58.

ten

Feasibility studies and the quantity surveyor and other consultants

Introduction

This chapter discusses the historical role of the quantity surveyor and shows how this has expanded from a passive role in the pre-contract process to embrace the more active role of a cost planner. The discussion will relate particularly to his changing role in the preparation of feasibility studies and possible improvements in his service. It will also discuss what a more refined approach means, distinguishing between the art and the science of cost planning.

Cost planning involves the use of the cost information, the basis of which are priced bills of quantities. Applying these costs to current proposals is part of the role of the QS in the feasibility study. As bills of quantities are central to the work of quantity surveyors, this chapter examines their use in deriving component costs.

The historical role of the quantity surveyor

The quantity surveyor's role has developed over the last two centuries, originating from measuring the completed work for the purpose of agreeing the payments between clients and builders. The client's demand for greater competitiveness and for more reliable forecasts of expenditure increased in the early nineteenth century. Quantity surveyors were employed to measure architects' drawings, and quantify and specify the work, prior to construction. Meanwhile groups of trades were joining together under one main contractor per job. The resulting bills of quantities could then be priced by each contractor, giving greater confidence and protection to both client and builder, concerning the basis of their agreement and construction costs.

The price information and expertise gained in the process led to the increased use of estimating prior to tendering. This developed in the 1960s onwards to cost planning methods which are geared to design purposes, more than construction purposes. Thus the role of the QS has evolved and he has been brought into the process at earlier stages from merely reporting after construction to forecasting and advising before design. This evolution continues as the QS can now use computer cost modelling methods such as Patterns and Spacewrapping, which are designed to evaluate building concepts.

Bills of Quantities

The priced bills of quantities gave the QS very powerful knowledge and helped develop his skill in understanding building costs, estimating and cost planning techniques. These techniques enable quantity surveyors to estimate the cost of construction during design. Chapters 5 and 6 show how these methods can be refined still further, with techniques designed to estimate at the earliest sketching stage or even prior to drawing work. The functions of a bill of quantities are to assist in the pricing and comparison of tenders, and to help reconcile and agree the costs of variations. These occur from the time of accepting tenders to the completion of construction. However, an accurately prepared bill has uses which go beyond this. Bills of quantities can be used to determine the quantities of building materials. They are the source from which construction cost analyses, element costs and component costs can be compiled as described in chapters 4 and 5, to use in feasibility studies and cost planning work.

The *Standard Method of Measurement for Building Works* ensures that bills of quantity in the United Kingdom are prepared on a common basis. This assists not only in the comparison of tenders for one job but also in the comparison of the prices of individual items.

Bills of quantities are usually comprised of sections which correspond closely to normal sub-contract packages. However, occasionally a trade bill for each major element, such as external walls and internal doors, is required. Bills of this form are used mainly to assist future cost planning. They have tended to be disliked by contractors because the same items appear in more than one element category, increasing the number of items to be priced. This should now be unnecessary, however, as computerised bills of quantities systems usually enable the same measurement to be sorted in to a conventional trade or elemental bill as required.

					£	
	Redland ridge and hip tiles to match roof tiles					
A	Half round ridge tiles with Dry Vent ridge system including PVC air flow control units, UPVC profile filler units, stainless steel batten fixing straps, ridge to ridge seals and fixing with stainless steel nails [9c]	142	m	£14.76	2095	92
B	Filled end (butt joint) with tile slips	7	Nr	£2.20	15	40
C	Mitred angle including inter-section with hip and valley	7	Nr	£4.00	28	—
D	Mitred angle including inter-section with 2Nr valleys	1	Nr	£4.00	4	—
E	Mitred angle including inter-section with hip and 2Nr valleys	2	Nr	£4.31	8	62
F	Intersection with hip	1	Nr	£3.78	3	78
G	Intersection with apex of 2Nr hips	19	Nr	£4.00	76	—
H	Three way intersection at apex of 2Nr valleys	2	Nr	£4.31	8	62
J	Intersection with apex of 2Nr valleys	19	Nr	£4.00	76	—
K	Intersection with hip and valley	1	Nr	£4.00	4	—
L	Third round hip tiles bedded in cement mortar (1:3) including filling pans of tiles with dentil slips [9d]	170	m	£7.42	1 261	40
M	Filled end with 6mm galvanised hip iron screwed to timber	58	Nr	£2.20	131	08
N	Junction with lower corner of gablet	12	Nr	£4.31	51	72
O	Fix lead soaker supplied by others [9g]	66	Nr	0.15	9	90

| 87/658 | | | 132 | | 3774 | 44 |

This means that a conventional trade bill may be prepared for pricing purposes, but when the prices are entered into the computer, the bill can be reformatted and priced in elemental form. Figure 10.1 shows a page from a typical bill of quantities. For the private QS, the priced bills of quantities remains the primary source of cost information.

Analysing costs

Cost data and analyses were discussed in chapters 4 and 5, where it was argued that the form of element and component cost data should be consistent from one job to the next. However, the price of the same component may differ on an office development compared to a housing project. This is because different varieties of work will attract different types of main contractors and sub-contractors. It is usually more accurate to use component data and adjust it depending on a particular market, building function or other factor, than to adjust an average elemental cost when different components are proposed. Having cost data is not enough; it is important to understand what the rates represent.

There are three types of price rates, derived from bills of quantities. *Elemental rates* provide the cost per unit for functional parts of buildings. Within each element, *component rates* are the cost per unit for each type of construction. *Bills of quantities rates* are the cost per unit of labour and materials for the finished work of each trade.

Deriving component rates from amplified analyses rather than using priced bills has several advantages. It saves time, when time can be least afforded during the cost planning stage. Using amplified analyses picks up items which might be overlooked, when assembling the cost of the composite item, such as reinforcement in a boundary wall, or various restraining bolts and straps.

An amplified analysis will take acount of the extent and effect of provisional sums and provisional quantities for each component. In total, the analysis of component costs should equal the tender price. This acts as a check on the compilation of the tender and that all figures are correct. Amplified costing can be easily integrated into cost libraries.

Where a QS practice deals with very diverse and complex building types it is not possible to compile a complete shopping list of components, which link to a single cost library, applicable to all projects. Component categories in its cost library may be broadened to embrace rather more

◀ **10.1** *Page from a typical bill of quantities*

variance in components. For example, polyester coated aluminium windows could be grouped together with anodised aluminium window types. Categories of cost may be similar to those described and costed in articles in the *Architects' Journal* under the heading of 'Design Data'.[1]

It may not be practical for QS practices to create cost libraries of component or element rates, if their volume of work is not great. In such circumstances early cost planning should be based on one or two analyses of projects for similar buildings. To obtain amplified cost analyses for these jobs as described in chapter 5, it would be necessary to define the component codes according to the most recent cost plan, which would then be used in the taking off process for bill production, and subsequent analysis.

Cost libraries

The co-ordination of analyses to a cost library can bring added advantages. In order to analyse data, one first has to bring cost rates to a common base to compare like with like. The rates have to be adjusted for time (using tender indices), and location (using location indices).

The adjustment of rates by indices uses the following formula:

$$\frac{\text{Updated Tender Index}}{\text{Original (or 'base') Index}} \times \frac{\text{Location Index for proposed scheme}}{\text{Location Index for original scheme}}$$

Moreover, the rates for certain items vary with size or quantity. For example, if the capacity of a heating system in one building were 75 kW, the rate per kW could not necessarily be applied to another system of 150 kW. This difficulty may be reduced by adjusting to one rate, based on a weighted average, for all buildings, equivalent to say a 100 kW system. The relationship between capacity and cost would still be required in the library in order to make the adjustments to the 100 kW rate in the future. One source of such cost and capacity relationships is the *Spon's Mechanical and Electrical Price Book*.

Having brought all the rates to a common base, the library will help to supply rates ready for use in computer cost models and other cost planning work. This reduces the amount of time required to estimate a specific job, giving a speedy response to the architect. The library also helps to overcome the problem of individual component price variability. Figure 10.2 shows an extract of an element and component cost library.

A major benefit is that by having the jobs on file in chronological order,

Do you wish rates to include preliminaries % ?   NO

Do you wish rates to include contingencies % ?   NO

	Maximum	Nr in Sam-ple	Average
Preliminaries	22.96	5	17.43
Contingencies	2.00	4	1.72

Element	Sub-Element	Code	Component, or specification choice.	Std Devi-ation	Min-imum	Max-imum	Sam-ple Nr	Unit of issue Nr	Qty	Average "All-in" Rate (excl Prelims and excl Conts). Tender index of 327.00
FIXED FITTING 2,079 4 1,845	KITCHEN FITTINGS	21. 1	Kitchen fittings:-B.D.C.cabinets "Henly" or similar	105.84	762	1,086	5	SETS		914.89
	COOKERS	2	Ariston fan oven with extract hood, and sealed hot plate			555	3	NR.		481.81
		3						NR.		
	HANDRAILS TO CORRIDORS	4	Handrails to corridors					M.		
	WARDROBES	5	Built-in mirror fronted wardrobes	24.59	211	280	5	NR		253.43
	SHELVES	6	Slatted shelving to airing cupboards	17.21	47	96	5	FLAT		67.85
	SUNDRY IRONMONGERY	7	Incl grab rails, h & c hooks, mirrors etc	13.56	47	86	5	FLAT		62.99
	FIRE EXTINGUISHERS	8	Fire extinguishers	36.71	29	115	5	FLAT		64.21
	PELMETS & CURTAIN BATTENS	9	Pelmets and curtain battens			24	2	FLAT		15.57
	TOWEL RAILS	10	Heated					NR.		
		11	Unheated					NR.		
FURNISHINGS	LOOSE	22. 1	Curtains							
SANITARY APPLIANCES 171.35 4 133.46	W.C.SUITE	23. 1	W.c.suite in coloured vitreous china, incl roll holder and grab rail	9.53	106	131	4	NR		121.59
	BIDETS	2	Bidets in coloured vitreous china.					NR		
	BATHS	3	1700mm in coloured U.P.V.C. acrylic bath incl.grab rails	34.09	169	256	4	NR		226.28
		4	1700mm bath in pressed steel incl grab rails					NR		
		5	1500mm sit-up bath, in pressed steel incl grab rails					NR		
	SHOWERS	6	Showers, incl. cubicle, pump, controls and b.w.i.c.	103.84	179	429	4	NR		310.92
	LAVATORY BASINS	7	Lavatory basins- in coloured vitrified clay	25.59	89	154	4	NR		110.29
	SINKS	8	Stainless steel single drainer sinks.	45.06	31	148	4	NR		74.51
DISPOSAL INSTALLATION 95.06 4 75.47	WASTE:APPLIANCE TO V.P.	24. 1	U.P.V.C. waste excl. vent pipes.	12.55	13.49	46.49	4	APPL.		28.66
	STACK VENT PIPES	24. 1	U.P.V.C. vent pipes rising through roof.	5.94	23.02	37.74	4	M.		27.53
		2	U.P.V.C. vent pipes terminating in one way valve in roof space			42.27	3	M.		26.02

10.2 Extract of Thamesdown cost library

it is possible to check the rate of tender price inflation against published data, and the effect of changes in specification and standards over time.

Preliminaries

This term has a very specific meaning when referring to construction projects. Preliminaries involve the work content and costs which are not directly related to specific construction activities, but to the essential supporting items. Most preliminaries can be grouped under four broad headings:

Supervision costs
Plant
Site set up and facilities
Insurances, etc.

Predicting the cost of preliminaries is the most difficult aspect of early estimating because the methods of construction and the specific requirements of a construction project can only be guessed. Many of these costs vary with time as well as the content of the rest of the work. They are often expressed in analyses as a percentage of the total tender price (less preliminaries and contingencies), and this percentage can vary enormously from 7 per cent to around 30 per cent.

Contractors' tender pricing policies vary from one contractor to the next. Some contractors add their preliminary costs to the cost of components, presenting, in their tender documents, 'all inclusive' rates for components. Other contractors may also include profits and office overheads within their bill rates. Still others may include profits and office overheads in a separate preliminaries section. It is not easy to interpret the pricing policies of contractors, who, understandably, will not usually be willing to discuss such matters.

Preliminaries are difficult to assess with any accuracy at an early stage, as plant used and the methods of construction cannot be readily predicted. However, a probable cost of preliminaries can be estimated by comparing a project with the sample of jobs in the surveyor's cost library, his store of cost information. The cost of preliminaries, may, or may not, be included in element and component rates. Ideally, from the library of cost information, it should be possible to calculate rates with or without preliminaries, as required. Component cost rates are usually more consistent and less variable, when preliminaries are excluded, than when they are included. Thus, where a QS can gain sufficient information and understanding to assess the cost of preliminaries with confidence, it is usually preferable to estimate them separately.

If the type of work varies substantially, each category of building, grouped according to function, should be kept separately in the library. However, shops may be grouped with offices, since they will attract similar main contractors and sub-contractors, working at comparable rates. Domestic construction, is a steadier, and lower risk market and rates will tend to be different than for say, offices.

The proportion of the cost of a building project attributable to preliminaries varies for a number of reasons including, the value of the rest of the work, access for deliveries, the use of cranes and plant, security problems especially on inner city sites and the general level of risk associated with a given project.

Data limitations: value of architecture

Even with all this cost information, it is important to take account of what cannot be expressed mathematically, namely the value of architectural merit. It is difficult to imagine any cost modelling system which can really evaluate this, but it must not be missed. There is often a great danger that profits depend largely upon figures such as the sales value per net square metre and other figures which are assessed in rather crude terms. It is sometimes hard to convince the valuer of the sales merit of certain architectural features. The conservative nature of the valuer's profession frequently discourages flair and individual style since this entails a risk for a cost. Surely some cost margin will nearly always be justified in order to achieve the something more than the achievement of a client brief in utilitarian terms only.

Data limitations: artistic or labour intensive work

Component data and cost libraries should be used with judgement, and with an understanding of their limitations. Labour intensive work, requiring high artistic or craft skill makes historic cost data very difficult to apply accurately. Such parameters would be near useless for work with a high degree of artistic content. For instance, one cannot estimate sculptures by Henry Moore in terms of cost per cubic metre for bronze, or the cost of a high quality oil painting in terms of cost per square metre.

Moreover, the use of data in this cost per cubic metre or area form has other limitations and must be used with caution. The method of valuing the cost of construction is costed using entities or components, rather than activities. This means that a component rate defines individual items and their cost, without taking particular circumstances into account. However, site storage facilities (which can be very important on tight urban sites), the positioning of a crane and many other factors relating to a specific site, will have a significant bearing on the total cost of construction quite apart from the cost of components. A practical limitation of conventional component costing techniques is the co-ordination of areas of surfaces and spaces with the size modules of components. For example, if a corridor uses suspended ceiling tiles of 600 mm square, then using a corridor width of say 1,220 mm (two tiles wide plus a tolerance) would avoid cutting and waste. If a corridor width were to be, say, 1,400 mm, more cutting and waste would be incurred. In fact, the extra cost may not be reflected in price, because of the short time available for tendering. For this reason, it is common for brick and blockwork construction, to make storey height modules a multiple of the height of a concrete block (225 mm). These practical implications are difficult to take into account at the feasibility stage as they involve a great deal of detail, which cannot usually be explored so early in a project.

Terms of appointment

The way that the QS carries out feasibility and cost planning work will often depend upon his terms of appointment. Quantity surveyors may, for instance, advise an unnecessarily high budget in order to reduce tensions in the subsequent design process and make cost planning easier. If he is also recommended by a friendly architect, he will be more likely to suggest a level of funding which will accord with the architect's wishes (depending, of course, on the personalities involved). This does at least help to ensure that the level of funding is realistic, and should help to avoid abortive design work in conjunction with cost cutting exercises. However, such an arrangement can result in unnecessarily expensive or even extravagent designs.

In theory, and in traditional practice, design control rests with the architect. The QS is the adviser on costs. However, the client frequently appoints the QS directly, and may place greater power and control in the QS's hands. The latter may be so concerned about controlling the design within the client's budget that broader implications may be overlooked. This can lead to difficulties in design and a lack of liaison.

Cost control requires knowledge, not only of costs but of the intricacies and complex interactions of a design. The cost planner therefore needs to be kept informed by the design team. In practice, however, consultants may not always inform the cost planner openly about their intentions. Where funding is restrictive the consultants may not wish to make their judgements explicit, for fear of giving the cost planner an opportunity to make savings in their section of the work. For example, extra costs may be required in order to meet a planner's requirements. The architect may foresee this before the cost planner, but if he is open about this possibility he risks other areas of the design having to be cut in order to remain within the budget. On the other hand, if he keeps his hunches to himself, he may succeed in persuading the client to increase the budget at a later stage of design, when it is too late to redesign to get the project back on budget, even before the construction phase.

In some instances, to avoid this situation, some clients will employ a separate QS for cost planning from the one advising on the budget. The chief disadvantage with this, is that, where one QS is involved in pre-contract work, he has the incentive to do each stage of work in a manner which makes the next stage easier. To employ a different QS can be wasteful of resources, as the QS, who carries out the cost planning work will duplicate the work already covered by the QS, who carried out the feasibility costings. Such an approach can be taken either as a poor reflection of the QS service, or as a sign of the mistrusting nature of the client.

Tight budgets

A QS may be appointed by a client to cost plan a project in accordance with a pre-determined budget and performance and quality standards. Occasionally, depending on how the initial budget was determined, it may be impossible to meet the performance and quality standards for the budgeted amount. In this situation, the QS's integrity and loyalties may be tested. To be fair to the design team and the ultimate users of the building, he should appeal to the client and explain the difficulty. This can be difficult professionally, since he may risk incurring the client's wrath. Yet a QS, who has carried out his research should not flinch from this, as he risks letting the design team and building users down, if he does not protest.

One of the major difficulties in questioning the client's budget is that while the cost planner is often able to foresee cost problems at an early design stage, the design may have to proceed much further before the point can be proved. By the time the design is firm enough to measure and confirm a cost forecast it is often too late to redesign and still meet construction deadlines. This situation frequently results in the substitution of poorer quality finishes and components in order to stay within budget limits. Avoiding this requires effective cost planning which once again, relies upon the trust, foresight and openness of the design team.

If the cost planner who sets the budget also does the cost planning, then sometimes many factors, which have a major cost impact, will have cover prices allocated to them. Paradoxically, if a client holds an inflexible view of early costings, then he will encourage a high estimate. The only way that the QS can avoid comebacks and cover items which have a cost risk is to increase his contingency allowances.

A QS will occasionally be required to estimate a tender within a prescribed margin of accuracy. This may be backed up by a penalty. For example, the terms of appointment may include a condition that if the tender figure varies from the estimate (prepared at scheme and estimate stage), by more than 7 per cent, then the cost planning fee will be halved.

Penalties as described above are often ineffective or unfair. If the tender comes in high, the QS may claim that items were introduced after the scheme and estimate stage. Arguments about the differences between the final drawings and those which formed the basis of the cost estimate are very common. It is unrealistic to expect a cost plan to be prepared so that the most detailed assumptions will be sufficiently explicit to refute any excuses which arise later. Such a penalty may create a defensive attitude, so that the QS will not report costs until the design is firmed up and he can feel confident. By this stage, the time for effective cost planning is usually past, and frequently time does not allow for redesign. When such terms are applied, most quantity surveyors will insist that they at least have the right to be consulted about the prospective list of contractors.

In theory, the application of penalties to encourage accurate estimates, can work. It does work for many clients. However, although practising the science of cost planning is not compromised, the art of cost planning becomes far more difficult. The art of cost planning is concerned with the interaction, communication and co-operation of the design team. The threat of sanctions hanging over the design and construction team can create a defensive approach, even encourage dishonesty and ultimately result in divisiveness in the building team. For example, if a QS is liable to lose his fee and yet is unable to persuade the project architect to make necessary savings, then he will need to report directly to the client although he would be most reluctant to do this, since such an action would discourage that architect from recommending him on any future job.

The role of the consultant engineers at the feasibility stage

Apart from an architect and quantity surveyor, lawyers and accountants also have a role to fulfil at an early stage in any building project. Other specialist consultants who may contribute to a feasibility study include mechanical engineers and structural engineers. For instance, the mechanical engineer loads the structure and puts holes in it, taking space in competition with the structure itself. He needs to know the use of the building, since its use determines services, air conditioning and heating requirements.

It is the mechanical engineer who will ultimately design and specify the heating system, not the quantity surveyor or any other member of the team. Therefore it is not enough that the cost model is acceptable on financial criteria; it has to be understood from each consultant's point of view. This can be achieved in the cost model with various sections for each consultant, such as structural, electrical and mechanical. Each consultant can then contribute their own judgements within their respective sections, even overriding the models default assumptions.

The work of the mechanical engineer will in turn affect the approach the structural engineer adopts. By involving structural engineers at an early stage, even before applying for planning permission, it is possible to save money and time, by producing the most appropriate structural solution. The structural engineer can consider alternative methods of building, including a flat or pitched roof, prefabrication or on site construction, and different materials such as brickwork, steel work, stone, or other cladding materials.

To the structural engineer, the critical factor is the soil condition, since foundations should be considered before structure. He is therefore in a position to take into account depth limitations at each floor level, various spacings, for example, the column beam grid spacing and any limitations on the number of storeys. To do this, the structural engineer should be brought in at the beginning. The key question is, what building is best suited to the soil?

Ground conditions determine the best use of resources, the type of foundations adopted and the number of columns in a structure. If piles are needed, the minimum number of piles would offer the most cost effective solution. To take full advantage of the piles, they should be sunk as deep as possible, since increasing the depth only adds slightly to the cost of piling. The extra cost of extending a pile is not as significant as sinking extra piles. Consequently, such structures should be built as high as possible rather than stretched across a site. Alternatively, foundations containing rafting or concrete plates often require the structure of buildings to be as low as possible, rarely over five floors.

Structural engineers may also advise on brickwork exteriors. For example, for single storey buildings such as sports halls, diaphram brick construction may be less costly than using a steel frame, since only one trade, bricklaying, is required to erect the structure. If often makes little economic sense to have a steel frame in such buildings as brickwork can be made load bearing. Though brickwork is slower to construct than other methods, it does not necessarily extend the construction period, as other work may be carried out simultaneously. However, an early roof may be required to beat winter weather conditions, for instance, and therefore call for a steel work erection. When brickwork is specified for aesthetic reasons, it is often advisable to use it as part of the load bearing structure. The aim is to exploit the load bearing capacity of resources as much as possible. High strength bricks should be used up to their maximum *permissible bearing pressure* (PBP). To reduce the cost of construction, the soil too, might be used up to its maximum, by making the foundations as small as possible without exceeding the PBP.

Advice from structural engineers at the beginning of a project can only contribute to the efficiency of proposals.

Feasibility costing in the United States

In the US there is no equivalent of the Royal Institute of Chartered Surveyors and according to KELLY and MALE, 'client accounting procedures do not allow easy computation of running costs and there are no standardised cost data banks, such as the BCIS'.[3] MORRIS reports: 'In the US market, using the traditional approach, the architect is generally responsible for construction cost estimating and for many architects this has proved to be an impossible task'.[4]

Most US building contracts are negotiated between developers and contractors directly and are generally bid on the basis of drawings and specifications. There are rarely any independent consultants for the engineering elements. According to CATT: ' . . . general contractors act as brokers in inviting sub-contractors to bid on plans and specifications as soon as the documents are issued. Once estimates are agreed a deal is struck between the parties to the contract. The architect remains on the sidelines'.[5] Understandably, according to MORRIS, when this approach is used the pre-tender period becomes protracted to enable the design to be firmed up.

Despite this, some organisations in the United States are practising many of the ideas of cost planning described in this book. In particular, *value management* (VM) embodies much of what is regarded in the United Kingdom as good cost planning. KELLY and MALE report, 'where possible VM consultants work from an elemental cost estimate and break this down into functions'.[3] However, it would appear that even where value management is employed, the lack of a widely accepted elemental system and data, limit the impact to later stages of design. Alternatively, the effective use of VM techniques often requires much design work to be undone. Some companies, such as HANSCOMB Associates[4] are improving on this situation, and produce cost analyses, use elaborate cost modelling systems, and in 1987, had a 35,000 item cost database.

Conclusion

The role and use of bills of quantities must not be underestimated. It is the most accurate provable evidence of prices paid and must be the backbone of a good cost library. The development and use of such a library can assist the client and design team to design cost effectively and avoid abortive work. The difference between traditional estimating and cost planning is that cost planning aims not only to get the costs right but to help to get the building right. Cost planning can be used to highlight and predict possible difficulties in time for consultants to take corrective action.

The client is more secure if one person can be responsible for both design and costs. The QS can never be responsible for design in the way that the architect should be. However, if the architect is to be responsible for design, quality, and consequential cost then he needs the help of the QS. The architect, who can produce good designs and understand building costs will be in a strong position to convince a client of the merits of a viable scheme. To do this he needs to adopt a teamwork approach, working in harmony with the other building professionals, including the quantity surveyor.

References

1. *Architects' Journal* 'Focus', April 1988 p 54.
2. *Spon's Mechanical and Electrical Price Book* 1989, Davis, Langdon and Everest, (Davis, Belfield and Everest, Quantity Surveyors until 1988).
3. KELLY, J and S MALE, 'Value Management and Quantity Surveying Practice', *Chartered Quantity Surveyor*, October 1987 pp 37–38.
4. MORRIS, MR, 'Inspiration for Quantity Surveying Diversification', *Chartered Quantity Surveyor*, November 1986 pp 23–25.
5. CATT, RICHARD, 'Quantity Surveying in Atlanta', *Chartered Quantity Surveyor'*, May 1987 pp 32–33.

eleven

Feasibility studies and the public enquiry

Introduction

In everyday life it is taken for granted that individuals may own and use their car to transport themselves from A to B. The cost of doing this, however, is shared between the car owner and the rest of the community. The cost to the individual is the capital cost of the vehicle, the cost of maintenance, tax, insurance and petrol. The cost to the rest of the community can be divided between other road users and the rest of society. The cost to other road users includes increased traffic congestion and added delays caused by the car's presence. Thus buses, cars and lorries take longer than they otherwise would to reach their destinations, and travelling time can be slowed down to such an extent that speeds in the capital's city centre streets is the same towards the end of the twentieth century as they were towards the end of the nineteenth. The costs to society as a whole can be seen in terms of the increase in noise and carbon monoxide pollution caused by the extra car, the extra risk of a traffic accident and the extra space needed to accommodate the vehicle, both when it is moving and when it is parked.

The total cost of an extra car to society is called the *social marginal cost* (SMC). The SMC is made up of the extra cost of the car to the individual, known as the *private marginal cost* (PMC) and the extra cost to the rest of society, which are called *external marginal costs* (EMC). Since there is no legal right to compensation for the inconvenience caused by a given vehicle, the EMC is ignored by individuals making decisions to purchase vehicles. However, their individual decisions may not serve the community's larger interests, even though the individual may perceive a personal gain from the acquisition. Hence, the car may be seen as the quickest and most convenient mode of transport, but if everybody were to travel by car the resulting congestion would slow all road users. It might be in everybody's interest to ban private vehicles in cities to enable public transport to move everybody far more quickly and efficiently (reducing pollution and the number and cost of accidents in the process).

The public enquiry

The public enquiry and the process of seeking planning permission is an attempt to include the EMC in the calculation of costs and benefits resulting from changes in the built environment. According to BALCHIN and KIEVE; 'Private development is essentially profit motivated. The unity of the environment and its quality, externalities and the interplay of social, political and economic factors will not be considered. A function of planning authorities is to make private developers bear some of the indirect costs created by imposing planning conditions'.[1] Indeed, in the United States developers are often called upon to provide roads and other environmental and infrastructure improvements in recognition of the extra costs their proposal would otherwise place on third parties.

Until the 1962 Town and Country Planning Act, planning permission once granted was difficult to reverse because the procedure involved the approval of the Secretary of State. The 1962 Act limited the period of time in which developers could take advantage of planning consent to five years, though compliance with this constraint was broadly defined. However, as LOMNICKI (1988) points out, if development is unduly and unjustifiably delayed, the planning authority may issue a 'completion notice' requiring the developer to carry out the construction within a stated time limit or permission would cease.[2] It is therefore essential to plan and manage the design and construction phases to demonstrate the nature of any delays that may arise. The feasibility study provides a comprehensive statement which achieves all three objectives, namely financial and economic planning, construction timing and gaining and defence of planning consent.

Since the 1968 Town and Country Planning Act, process planning, which sees planning as an interactive process between a building proposal and its environment, has involved taking into account social and economic factors. Earlier, blueprint planning, which made use of a predetermined set of planning tools, had sought planning consistency largely by referring to land-use maps and building controls.

The Local Government, Planning and Land Act of 1980 relaxed planning controls by enabling the Secretary of State for the Environment to create *Enterprise Zones*. The Housing and Planning Act of 1986 developed the concept of Enterprise Zones into Simplified Planning Zones, further reducing the complexity of the planning procedures for potential developers, wishing to build within the zones' boundaries. The 1986 Act also amended several clauses in the Town and Country Planning Act of 1971, including controls on demolition in conservation areas, local enquiries and the procedure on appeals, where no local inquiry may have taken place as well as the determination of appeals by inspectors.

Larger projects especially, may have a major impact upon a variety of social or environmental factors. Considerations which are dealt with through the local authority planning process may include overall size, area of building on ground, height, shape, rights of light, materials used, landscaping, car parking provision, density on site, access and wider effects on transport routes, environmental factors such as a sewage embargo, or limits on emission of effluents.

Planning permission must be sought from the local authority, through its planning committee, composed of locally elected councillors. They may grant permission, stipulate conditions or refuse to give permission for a proposed development. If permission is refused, then the developer may appeal. An inspector is then appointed to conduct a public enquiry into the proposed scheme. It has become increasingly important to recognise the right of members of the general public to object to proposed schemes and participate in the planning process. Perhaps this is as it should be in a democratic society. With growing experience and knowledge of public enquiries, organisations concerned with the environment, recreation and conservation have begun to succeed in influencing the siting and scale of developments in many areas. This is a vital activity as clearly many interests, often in conflict with each other, have to be considered and not only those of the developer.

The theoretical economic framework of public enquiries into construction proposals identifies the questions and difficulties which need to be resolved. Namely, who are the direct and indirect beneficiaries and losers of a scheme and what are the values associated with their gains and losses? In chapter 1, PARETO optimality described one economic objective of changes in society. It is the aim of the enquiry to establish that it is not possible to increase welfare by a further distribution of resources. Clearly there are real difficulties in establishing PARETO optimality, since comparisons between the welfare of individuals are impossible to make.

The HICKS–KALDOR test attempts to resolve this difficulty by requiring, in theory, those who gain from a change to compensate those who lose. This could only apply where the value of the gains was greater than the value of losses. Unfortunately this criterion also ignores the distribution of gainers and losers. Since wealthier people are likely to lose more in monetary value than poor individuals, compensation to wealthier individuals would tend to be greater under this system. However, the greatest losers may be the poorest, whose loss of small amounts will mean more to them than the losses to the wealthy.

The SKITOVSKY double criterion requires that two conditions be met. The first is the HICKS–KALDOR test, which examines values assuming a change were to take place. However, the second condition assumes the project does not go ahead.

First condition; if project goes ahead, value of gains greater than value of losses. Project is acceptable.

Second condition; if project were not to go ahead, value of potential gains should be greater than value of the current position to potential losers. Project is acceptable.

The SKITOVSKY double criterion requires the project to be acceptable on both criteria. As neither condition takes the distribution of income and wealth into account, I M D LITTLE has suggested that the re-distribution of wealth resulting from a change should tend to favour of the poor rather than the rich to increase welfare in society.

A well researched feasibility study will have anticipated the difficulties of measuring the subjective valuations of spillover effects, sometimes called external economies or diseconomies, depending on whether or not they are seen as beneficial or detrimental. It is therefore the duty of the writer of feasibility studies to prepare the client for such objections, which might be put to a public enquiry and potentially delay the start of a project. The study must allow for the cost of the solutions as well as the cost of any delays that may be incurred. Similarly a feasibility study prepared for opponents of a scheme should take into account the developer's financial interest in the proposal and their alternative solution should also be economically viable.

In spite of the difficulties of quantifying intangible costs and benefits, if adequate allowance has been made then the objectivity of the public enquiry may be appealed to on the grounds of a balanced argument in favour of (or against) a particular proposal. This may sound like sophistry or an attempt to hoodwink the public enquiry but unless the arguments are convincing, those holding an opposing viewpoint will be able to stress that specific weakness in the report.

Environmental, urban and economic impact analyses

The purpose of Environmental Impact Analysis (EIA), is to present the arguments for and against specific projects to enable a balanced decision to be made. Similarly, Urban Impact Analysis (UIA), is concerned with the effects of policies rather than specific building proposals. MASSEY points out that; 'The real methodological problems facing successful urban impact analysis are those of sensitive and thoughtful conceptualisation rather than those of a search after a (probably spurious) quantitative rigour'.[3] Complex statistical presentations including esoteric economic calculations often only lead to a justifiable scepticism regarding the conclusions.

EIA has been developed in the United States to account for the effects of proposals of Federal Government agencies on the ecology of an area. Beneficial changes to the environment may lead to improved health of the population, increased use and enjoyment of the natural amenities in a locality for recreation purposes and the stability and diversity of the ecosystem. There may also be wider effects on visibility and the weather.

An EIA report is used only if significant physical changes to the environment are anticipated as well as social and economic impacts. In 1981, for the purpose of stating when an EIA was required by law, the US Government defined a significant effect on the economy as an economic impact valued at at least $100 million per annum. Although the value of the economic and environmental impacts of the vast majority of construction projects will tend to be far less than £100 million per annum, similar principles may be applied to provide a useful framework for discussion at public enquiries. A narrow financial appraisal which included only direct costs incurred by the developer may ignore the far greater costs incurred by society or the environment in the longer term. One reason for this is that there may be no legal obligation on the developer to compensate others for loss of amenity or pollution. Yet often projects impose such costs on the surrounding population and ecology. Because of the pressures of competition, firms often find it necessary to keep financial costs to a minimum and government intervention may be needed in the form of planning constraints and conditions to protect the wider interests of society and the environment. The extra costs imposed on the developer must therefore be weighed against the extra gains accruing to society by the imposition of these restrictions.

The National Environmental Policy Act of 1969 and the Office of Management and Budget Directive A107 required economic and environmental impact studies to be carried out. Executive Order 12291, which was issued by President Reagan in 1981 reinforced the earlier measures. United States' legislation states that, 'all agencies of the Federal Government (to) ... include in every recommendation or report on proposals for legislation and other major federal actions significantly affecting the quality of the human environment, a detailed statement by the responsible official on . . .

(i) The environmental impact of the proposed action.

(ii) Any adverse effects which cannot be avoided should the proposal be implemented.

(iii) Alternatives to the proposed action.

(iv) The relationship between local short-term uses of man's environment and the maintenance of long-term productivity.

(v) Any irreversible and irretrievable commitments of resources which would be involved in the proposed action should it be implemented.'[4]

While such an approach may not always be applicable or possible in the United Kingdom, the points raised are or could be relevant issues confronting major projects at public enquiries.

Often various groups affected by a proposal will have been approached during the period of investigation for an EIA and in the process of preparing the document many of the anticipated difficulties will have been ironed out leaving only the unresolved differences to be settled by the enquiry. In this way EIAs may in fact save time and costs for the developer, other interested parties and the authorities. The final report is a systematic document which highlights the disputes and concentrates attention on the major issues.

Much of the information contained in EIAs is found by reference to expert witnesses. Other information such as values associated with certain implications may be negotiated between the interested parties and the consultants carrying out the appraisal. According to HALL; 'There is an intrinsic difference between impact analysis on the one hand, and assessment or evaluation on the other . . . Many of the methods of EIA . . . fundamentally involve systematic checklists of impacts which are themselves not comparable . . . EIA is a useful additional battery of techniques that can aid the planner – and also the political decision maker and the affected public – to conduct a more rational, more structured debate about the effects of proposals for development, and about the weights that ought to be attached to these effects'.[5] The EIA simply attempts to combine arguments and give them relative weights. The problem arises as to which impacts should be included and which ignored by an EIA. THIRLWELL proposes that; 'the authority responsible for deciding whether an analysis was required . . . should determine what environmental impacts were relevant to a particular planning decision and should therefore be included in the impact analysis'.[6]

Since intangible costs and benefits are drawn into feasibility studies, many economists argue that it is useful to include valuations of these in the calculations of present values and rates of return. Naturally, many intangible costs and benefits will be involved and finding agreement between the various parties requires understanding, interpretation and tact. A summary of the techniques employed to establish the values associated with certain intangible costs will demonstrate the broad approaches which might be taken and applied to any feasibility study. The approaches are necessarily flexible to allow for adaptation to particular circumstances. It is always essential to interpret results. Their significance depends on the assumptions used to estimate the values of the variable inputs. Once a value has been established, that figure is then fed in to the calculations along with the tangible costs and benefits.

Where only one intangible cost or benefit remains to be calculated, the following methods may be applied. One approach to estimating a value for an intangible cost is to calculate the maximum value which will still permit the project to continue, namely the value which would still produce a sufficiently high social rate of return. Similarly, the value of an intangible benefit may be assessed by calculating the minimum value of the benefit which will produce an acceptable social rate of return.

Another approach is to attribute a value to the intangible cost or benefit and using the same value, apply the figure to each option in turn, using the usual discounting calculations to find the NDPVs of each option. This process can be repeated using sensitivity analysis, to find if the value, when raised or lowered, is significant in altering the order of preference of the options.

Other techniques have been used to find values for specific intangible costs and benefits. One example of an intangible cost or benefit is the value of human life. In some instances, human life may be seen as a cost of a project. The value of a life is implied by the expenditure on safety precautions divided by the number of lives risked and the reduced probability of an individual's death. In other cases, human lives may be considered as a gain, for instance, the number of extra people likely to be saved by the improvement to hospital facilities in an area. Although there are moral objections to such an evaluation, it is nevertheless implied by or assumed in many of the decisions to spend money to save a life or even to risk one.

One method used to establish the value society attaches to life is to find the extra paid to people working in occupations with a greater risk of death, such as oil rig workers, compared to other jobs with lower risks, such as sailors, with similar qualifications and experience. According to studies carried out in the United States, MERKHOFER notes that 'riskier jobs have annual wages that are between $4 and $70 higher for each 1 in 100,000 increase in the rate of mortality'.[7] These apparently small amounts clearly become significant when the total numbers employed in an industry or even within a factory are multiplied by the extra wages which must be paid to compensate for the extra risk associated with the job. Measures, which reduce the risk element of a job can then be set against the savings in wages in the long run. The value of a human life implied by the above figures varied from $400,000 to $700,000. Similar valuations can be applied to improving safety even in non-working environments, such as shopping malls and railway stations.

An alternative method for evaluating human life, the human capital approach, considers each life as an asset. The value of a life is the present value of the individual's future earnings, assuming this to be their economic contribution to society. This method has obvious difficulties, since many people are not wage earners and those who are may not continue to earn the same amounts until retirement.

Other methods used for dealing with the issue of human life valuation, do so by leaving the human factor till last. In a hospital project for example, find the minimum value of a life that would be necessary to make the proposal viable, using net present values. In other circumstances, when risking human life may be seen as a cost to a project such as an oil rig, find the maximum value of a life that would render the scheme unacceptable. A similar technique, sugested by MERKHOFER, is to assign values to life, ranging perhaps from $200,000 to $4 million and finding out how sensitive the project is to particular valuations. BENTKOVER describes yet another method of evaluating not only human life but also injury and disability by reference to the avoided cost, which may be stated in monetary terms or in terms of for instance avoided pain in the event of an injury. Although this method and the two preceding techniques may appear callous, materialistic and simplistic, they do not actually assert that a human life is in fact only worth the stated figure but that, for the project to go ahead or be rejected, an assumption about the value of human life, amounting to the stated figure, is implied by the decision.

The value of an amenity may also be measured at least indirectly, by considering the travelling time and cost involved in reaching its location. The travel costs are an indication of the value people attach to visiting the amenity, such as a national park. The more the amenity is valued, the further will people be willing to travel to visit it. Questionnaires may be used on a random sample of visitors, asking them to state the distance travelled to reach the amenity, the mode of transport used and whether or not they would still be willing to visit the locality given the effect of the proposed change to the environment. This data may be used to form the basis of estimating the drop in the amenity value by measuring the drop in the value of journeys taken to visit the site or locality.

It is recognised by ecologists as well as many economists and increasingly realised in political circles that industrial pollution caused either by economic growth or increased numbers of visitors, which disregards the impact on the environment, will be counter-productive in the long run. This view is supported by BALCHIN and KIEVE who maintain that; 'The environmental argument must be continuously brought into the balance sheet'.[8] Legislation such as the Control of Pollution Act, 1974 also reinforces this view. The LEITCH Committee set up by the Department of Transport in 1977 to assess trunk roads suggested that environmental considerations should play a major part in appraisals. Planning Programming Budgeting Systems (PPBS), attempt to deal with proposals in the context of environmental and human factors as well as purely physical needs.

The cost of pollution may be considered in terms of the cost of avoiding the effects together with a valuation of individuals inconvenience and distaste for the pollution. The cost of avoiding the effects of pollution may be seen in terms of the amount needed for the measures which would have to be taken to avoid the pollution occurring in the first place. Alternatively, the valuation of the pollution may be assessed by examining the cost of moving people to new homes away from the polluted areas, one method of valuation used by the nuclear waste industry. However, it is widely appreciated that the cost of pollution extends far beyond the area of immediate environmental impact. Damage caused by pollution is often very long lasting and dangerous and frequently requires expensive security measures. Where there is only a risk of pollution then the value of the damage multiplied by the probability of that level of damage occurring will produce a distribution of the likely values to be avoided by extra spending on safety measures.

The value of intangible costs and benefits have to be considered throughout the life of a project and sometimes, even after the project has ceased to operate as in the case of nuclear power stations. However, a problem emerges as to what is the correct discount rate to use. D W PEARCE takes, for example, an investment such as a nuclear power station, which is designed to function for fifty years. After its operating life it is expected to continue to cause environmental damage and incur expenses in order to maintain security on the site. Suppose that these future costs are £1 m per annum in perpetuity, the present value of these distant-future costs discounted at 10 per cent is only £85,000. In other words the power station would only need to generate a net present value of £85,000, equivalent to a trading surplus of only £8,600 per annum, for the project to be viable. This result may or may not be acceptable to the decision makers or the public enquiry, but it does highlight the problem of discounting enormous costs which will only be incurred in the distant future. The small present value may not reflect the importance attached to future environmental damage, which it is not intended to belittle.

Conclusion

Several approaches have therefore been taken concerning the appropriate discount rate to apply to intangible costs, especially when these costs and benefits extend well into the future across generations. One view is to use a low discount rate on intangibles to take into account that there is a time preference as well as the possibility of using a sinking fund to ameliorate the distant future adverse affects of a proposal. Another view considers that since discounting even at low rates of discount will tend to underestimate the future values of intangible costs, they should not be discounted at all. Furthermore, as natural amenities and resources relative to population will tend to decline, their relative value in the long run will tend to rise. By simply not discounting assumes that the increased real value has to some extent been cancelled out in the calculations.

It must be understood that the values attached to intangibles which any enquiry uses are not as important as the process of establishing the figures, since it is the process itself which highlights the difficulties in coming to a conclusion and making final decisions on proposals. The debate at a public enquiry is then concentrated on interpreting the results and making qualitative judgements about the conclusions. The figures presented do not substitute for human decision making but only assist in understanding the magnitude of some of the consequences implicit in the choices which are made. The interests of the developer are then seen in the context of conflicting interests, attitudes and in society.

References

[1] BALCHIN, PN and JL KIEVE, *Urban Land Economics*, (2nd ed) Macmillan 1982 p 88

2 LOMNICKI, A, 'Abandoned Planning Permissions,' *The Law Magazine*, The Department of Estate Management, South Bank Polytechnic, 1988 pp 4–10

3 MASSEY, D, 'Urban Impact Analysis: the Potential for its Application in the UK,' *Built Environment*, Vol 6 No 2, 1980 p 133

4 STOEL, TB, JR and SJ SCHERR, 'Experience with EIA in the United States,' *Built Environment*, Vol 4 No 2 June 1978 p 94

5 HALL, P, 'Environmental Impact Analysis – Scientific Tool or Philosopher's Stone?' *Built Environment*, Vol 4 No 2 June 1978 p 86

6 THIRLWELL, G, 'EIA – Taking Stock,' *Built Environment*, Vol 4 No 2 June 1978 p 88

7 MERKHOFER, MW, *Decision Science and Social Risk Management*, D Reidel Publishing Company 1987 p 98

8 BALCHIN, PN and JL KIEVE, ibid p 183

twelve

Interpreting feasibility studies

Introduction

Before using any technique it is important to appreciate its limitations. Every method and model described in this book may only be used under certain circumstances to answer specific questions, depending on the assumptions made and the information available. Judgement is therefore required to select the most appropriate approach. The techniques do not form a substitute for human judgement but are designed only as an aid to decision making.

In this chapter, various theoretical objections to, and some practical limitations of, feasibility studies are introduced. Only when these limitations are recognised, can the results of calculations, the cost figures themselves, be interpreted with any sensitivity.

Problems of measurement

Problems of measurement arise out of the difficulty of finding accurate information. It is rarely a matter of measuring areas directly as the cost of gathering the raw data would be a costly exercise. Indeed it can be argued that the technique is hardly scientific, because the input data cannot be observed, since it is data of previous projects or general data applied to a proposal yet to be built. It is not possible to produce accurate costs from incomplete designs. Nevertheless, the information forms the basis of the assumptions upon which practical decisions are taken.

It is often considered by those conducting feasibility studies, that only those costs with a financial tag may be included in the financial appraisal of a scheme. However, it is often those costs for which no money changes hands which form the most important elements in terms of costs and benefits. These intangible costs, including the value of life, the value of a healthy environment and the price of freedom may all be difficult to

168

measure but if they are not included in the calculations of NPV and IRR, there is a tendency to ignore them.

At the same time, it is important to realise that the value associated with financial transactions, the tangible costs and benefits of a scheme may not necessarily reflect the value of the cost or benefit to society. Thus, the price of a theatre seat may be an understatement of its value to theatre-goers. The excess value, which is not accounted for in the price is known as consumer surplus. This surplus value is the difference between the price paid and the price the purchaser would have been willing to pay. Individual consumer surpluses should be included in the valuation of the benefit to building users. However, the distribution of income in society may also affect the valuation of benefits, if the benefits to society are taken to be worth only what those fortunate enough to be able to afford theatre tickets paid together with their aggregate consumer surplus. This assumes the status quo is desirable and discourages developments with an element of redistributing income from the wealthier strata of society to the less well off.

The benefits of hospitals include the price paid for medical treatment and consumer surpluses, which provides an evaluation of the hospital service to the individuals who benefit. However, there is a further round of benefits to society at large, as treated individuals are returned to their work place to continue as productive members of the community.

Problems of prediction

Making predictions about future events and trends is always a hazardous occupation. Nevertheless, it is necessary to anticipate future costs and benefits associated with buildings for up to sixty years, the expected useful designed life of many building projects.

In order to overcome the uncertainty about future trends, sensitivity analysis may be used. This permits various scenarios concerning the future to be calculated by seeing what would happen if future figures were increased or lowered by various percentages. Thus, for instance, if costs were to be raised by 10 per cent or revenues lowered by 15 per cent, the NPV could be calculated for each case in turn. A frequency distribution of NPVs would show the modal or most common NPV, when variables are altered from one scenario to the next. These trials can be conducted by computers almost automatically using what are known as *Monte Carlo techniques*, so called because of the laws of probability and the number of scenarios or chances which are generated. As many variables as desired may be given ranges within which the final figure is most likely to lie. The computer then generates a series of scenarios for each required interval of the range. This process quickly generates thousands of scenarios, which produce a distribution of results. These techniques can be used on all options and the resulting graphs will produce risk profiles, which can then be used to compare proposals.

Problems of costing

Costing projects involves including certain costs and excluding others. Often, the costs which are ignored are important variables, but the problem is that the analysis of costs and benefits is of necessity only a partial analysis. It is simply not possible to take into account all the costs and benefits arising out of a project, since many of these will be widespread, unmeasurable and uncertain, even extending into neighbouring countries. While estimates may be possible in theory, many relatively small projects would not justify the expense of the investigation, of what would in any case, only be the marginal effects of a given scheme.

At the inception stage, it is usually advisable on all but the simplest of projects for the quantity surveyor or architect to report only a likely range of costs. The difficulty of placing a monetary value against costs and benefits arises in part because the measuring yardstick itself suffers from a loss in purchasing power over time caused by inflation.

Building inflation from the time a budget is set to tender date is hard to predict, particularly for long contracts in periods of high inflation. Some local authorities and many companies relieve their design teams of this risk, by setting the budget at an historical base date and calculate the revised budget at the time of tender. By this time, published indices will enable tender price inflation to be calculated more accurately than when looking forward in time. The indices are only indicators of average price increases and as such may not necessarily be accurate for a particular scheme or set of circumstances.

Different groups place different values on identical notional costs and benefits. Such disputes are impossible to resolve. As a result, feasibility studies will tend to represent the values of the sponsor of the study rather than third parties. Such a bias will tend to diminish the usefulness of feasibility studies in reaching objective conclusions. Certainly, sensitivity analysis may be used to test different valuations of specific costs and benefits. If a higher or lower valuation by a third party does not destroy the viability of a project then it could be argued that the project could still proceed. However, even where the third party valuation interferes with a project's returns, judgement would still be required to decide whether such a value is indeed any more valid than presumably the promoter's own valuation which made the project financially acceptable. For this reason public enquiries are important administrative devices for judging and resolving such arguments. Compensating one group for losses incurred due to another group gaining benefits means that there is a tendency to defend the status quo. In reality many projects, especially public sector projects such as Enterprise Zones in depressed areas, may be deliberately designed to redistribute income in society. Any compensation will tend to reduce the extent of redistribution.

Problems of discounting

Discounting techniques create problems as the rate of discount used to establish present values is itself an arbitrary figure. Nevertheless, the figure chosen will determine not only the present value but also the period over which the future flows of spending and income remain significant for decision making purposes.

Moreover, the discount rate assumes that money is set aside in the present period to accrue to the future value at a given discount rate, although interest rates change from time to time. This variation in interest rates will in turn invalidate the assumptions made when discounting, the chief of which is that interest rates remain constant between the present and a given year or month in the future. The rate of inflation will also tend to reduce the purchasing power of future sums of money. The real rate of interest, which is the difference between the nominal interest rate and the rate of inflation will also tend to fluctuate, but this fluctuation is relatively low.

The correct discount rate to use is often seen as a contentious issue, especially on public sector projects. In fact, the issue can be avoided to some extent by finding the internal rate of return. If social costs and benefits have been included in the analysis, the social rate of return will show a rate which may be used to compare options in the public sector. The difference between social time preference and the market cost of borrowing or the opportunity cost of foregone private investment, is usually minimal and would in any case lend spurious accuracy to any conclusions. In practice, as noted in chapter 8, the net return on private investment on equivalent projects, or even the weighted average rate of return would be suitable approximations for a target rate of return in the public sector.

Unrealistic assumptions

It may be necessary to make several unrealistic assumptions in the course of conducting a feasibility study. These assumptions may invalidate some of the study's conclusions, if viewed as significantly at variance with the particular circumstances of a given project. The conditions assumed may include the following statements:

(a) Interest rates are unaffected by the project.

(b) Exchange rates are unchanged by the drain on foreign currency reserves.

(c) Local construction material prices and wages do not rise as a result of the impact of the increased workload of a proposed project on an area.

FELDSTEIN makes the following assumptions:

1   Resources are fully employed and prices are stable.

2   Small redistributions of income leave social welfare unchanged.

3   All magnitudes are known with certainty.

4   Commodity markets are perfect so that market prices reflect social costs.

5   There are no collection costs or deadweight losses associated with tax revenues.

6   There is no external borrowing.[1]

Difficulties of application

There are several distinct areas in which problems may arise when applying the methods advocated in this book to particular construction projects. These are problems of management, the quality or reliability of cost information, the measurement and weighting of spillover effects and, finally, the development and maintenance of models and technical, support generally.

Management problems are derived from the fact that most major clients are a combination of separate departments. The various departments may not understand or co-operate with each other. Frequently, there is no one individual with responsibility for all decisions, taking an overall view. Moreover, few clients carry out life cycle costing.

Even within the design and construction team individual value judgements about design priorities are required. For instance, should a budget be increased, or should the finishes specification or the standard of air treatment be reduced? Each consultant will tend to argue the case for maintaining standards in his area of responsibility.

The quality of cost data depends on effective feedback. Using bills of quantities and cost analyses can refine costing, based on empirical evidence rather than supposition and subjective judgements. This method requires co-operation between the bill production team and those who carry out feasibility and cost planning work.

The measurement of spillover effects relies on the judgement of the decision maker, with the help of his advisers. The results of questionnaires invariably require interpretation. Moreover, even if the values of a particular affect were accurately evaluated, it would still be necessary to consider the distribution of the cost or benefit on different groups in society. Often, arbitrary methods are adopted for allocating intangible costs and benefits between conflicting parties. In any case, a given distribution may be impossible to test or verify.

Fortunately, these problems can be overcome if they are understood by all parties. The figures and patterns of distribution are all assumptions. As decisions will always involve implicit assumptions, it will often be useful to make these explicit in order to discuss and judge the merits of choices.

Risk

The subject of risk analysis cannot be dealt with adequately within the scope of this book. Nevertheless, it is important to recognise that many factors have an influence on design and cost which are largely beyond the influence of the specific design. Furthermore, their extent cannot always be ascertained in the early design stages, for instance, uncertainty will surround sales or rental values.

Factors, which are variable and entail risk, which cannot reasonably be limited or avoided should be defined. Limits might be set against the likely cost variability of these factors. Risk factors may be taken to include particular turbulent market factors which may affect tenders, such as the number of projects being considered at any one time. The cost of many abnormal items or construction problems cannot be easily ascertained from any historical cost library.

A checklist of 'abnormals' or construction risk factors might include the following: difficult access, overhead power cables, slope of ground, soft ground needing piling, clay soil requiring extra drainage, acidic soil needing protection or sulphate resisting cement, working close to existing buildings, work to boundaries, restrictions on making noise, accessibility of main services, possible financial contribution to drainage authorities for connections to sewers, demolition, and work below ground water table level or work restricted by tides if a site is near a tidal river.

It is necessary to strike a balance between rejecting viable projects and accepting others which are not viable. Moreover, when carrying out a residual valuation for land evaluation, a budget which accounts for the most pessimistic outcome of all factors at risk would result in very few land bids being successful.

Calculating a net present value or an internal rate of return does not indicate the probability of the figures being correct. A distribution of the mean and standard deviation of the net present values associated with a given project might be used to show the risk of a scheme when the values of the variable input are altered. One standard deviation above and below the average or arithmetic mean is the range within which two out of every three results should fall. The range between two standard deviations above and below the mean contains approximately 19 out of 20 results, implying 95 per cent confidence limits. The distribution of one option might then be compared to the distribution of an alternative. The higher the standard deviation of the distribution the greater the expected risk of the option and the higher the minimum acceptable rate of return.

A recognised statistical method for comparing risk is the coefficient of variance. This measures the standard deviation as a proportion of the average. Thus, if the distribution of the results of changing the variables of one option has a standard deviation of £1 m and an average net present value of £10 m, its coefficient of variation of 0.1. If an alternative scheme offered a standard deviation of £2 m and an average net present value of £15 m, its coefficient of variance is 0.13. The option with the lower coefficient of variance, therefore offers the lower risk.

It is important to have data which is not only informative, but verifiable and capable of explanation. Computerised techniques in which the logic is hidden in a 'black box'and rely on statistical theories may be very limited, and should be used with caution. According to RAFFERTY, some of the Monte Carlo simulation estimating techniques expounded in the mid-1980s fall into this category.[2]

Analysing each large risk by splitting it down into several smaller risks may overlook various combinations of factors. Frequently, design disasters occur through the combination of circumstances or the failure of a component or element, which was simply not imagined during design. It is possible that the same things which have been overlooked in the design will also be overlooked in the risk study and maintenance forecast. Feasibility studies must oversimplify the cost implications of component failures, which often entail significant future expenses. These failures often involve complex interactions as one component failure often adversely affects other components, inconveniencing the building users and damaging equipment and furnishings.

Operating perspective

So great are the uncertainties and risks that one school of thought suggests that randomising the figures in bills of quantities would hardly make a significant difference to their usefulness as predictors of building costs. Indeed, different firms of quantity surveyors use different techniques to cost projects with different results. Nevertheless, in spite of the difficulties referred to above, managements expect and require assistance and advice in making decisions. They require consistency, rationality and account-ability. Feasibility studies offer a systematic approach to decision making, allowing managers to consider many different aspects of the choices confronting them. In the final analysis, a decision involves judgement, including the decision maker's subjective preferences, tastes and attitude towards risk.

References

[1] FELDSTEIN, MS, *The Inadequacy of Weighted Discounted Rates, in Cost Benefit Analysis*, ed R Layard, PenguinBooks 1972 p 312.
[2] RAFFERTY, J, The State of Cost/Price Modelling in the UK Construction Industry: A Multicriteria Approach, *Building Cost Modelling and Computers*, Spon 1987.

thirteen

A worked example

The following is an account based upon a recent study for a primary school.

Inception

An independent preparatory school was in a poor state of repair, but the possibility of relocating to a new site was under consideration with the prospect thereby of gaining from the latent value of their existing land. The school had little capital available and would only be able to pay back loans at the maximum of £20,000 to £25,000 per year.

The school's main asset was the existing site. This was on level ground in a desirable area, close to shops and facilities. The trustees were aware that the site was very suitable for a sheltered housing development. They understood that similar sites had attracted high bids from such developers. The trustees therefore authorised that developers be approached to invite bids for the land, and that an alternative site be sought.

An alternative site was found in a more rural location, costing £600,000, and a bid of £1,300,000 was received from a sheltered housing developer for their existing land. The school therefore decided to commission a feasibility study to evaluate its best course of action.

Objectives and user needs

A new replacement school needed to cater for a maximum of 180 pupils. The pupil/teacher ratio was higher than in the state system generally, and the maximum number of pupils in each classroom was as follows:

Nursery (3–4 years old)	Maximum 18 in 1 room
Infants (5–7 years old)	Maximum 24 per room in 3 rooms
Juniors (8–11 years old)	Maximum 28 per room in 4 rooms.

Following consultation between the head, staff and the design team, it was judged that the design should aim to allocate a similar area per pupil at each age group. The reason for this was that whilst smaller children would appear to need less space, in fact they need as much as older children because they are more active.

In order to help ascertain space requirements an area analysis was carried out on the existing accommodation, as shown in figure 13.1. This was compared with area standards used for budgeting in a county council. From these area analyses, and through consultation, a schedule of areas was proposed which formed a major part of the client brief.

Layout of the building

The nursery and infant classrooms were to be arranged in a semi-open plan (in building terms, not fully enclosed). The junior classrooms, however, were to be fully enclosed in the traditional manner, served by corridors.

The client had been advised that it would be cheaper to have at least part of the building rising to two storeys and wished to investigate this against a single storey option. Depending on cost constraints, it was thought that the form should be a courtyard scheme of a span of approximately 9 metres. This figure, plus the figures for floor areas and storey heights for each level, was sufficient information to calculate the area of the external envelope of the building.

Specification standards

The specification standards were defined in terms of performance standards and components. Examples of these requirements were as follows:

All classrooms were to have a sink. The numbers of toilets and basins to correspond to the standards recommended by the Department of Education and Science (DES).

Other requirements included:

Walls: brickwork and blockwork with insulated cavity.

Windows: robust, possibly hardwood or galvanised steel.

A Worked Example

NAME - Proposed school

DESCRIPTION -   8 bases for 3 to 11 year olds

					Areas	Section Sub totals
1 TEACHING	Nursery	1 base at	36.0	:	36.0	
	Infants	3 bases at	40.0	:	120	
	Juniors	4 bases at	43.0	:	172	
	Extra multi-purpose base	1 base at	40.0	:	40	
	Music tuition room			:	9.0	
	Hall and stage			:	205.0	
	Library			:	14.0	596
2 STORAGE	In teaching bases	8 bases at	3.00 m2 each	:	24.0	
	P.E			:	11.0	
	Dining / chairs store			:	20.0	
	Stock room			:	8.0	
	Other			:	15.0	78
3. PUPIL'S CHANGING & TOILETS	Cloaks	4 bases at	2.00 m2 each	:	8.0	
	Toilets	11 cubicles at 2.15 m2 each		:	23.7	
	Changing			:	30.0	62
4 ADMINISTRATION	Head			:	13.0	
	Secretary			:	13.0	
	Staff room			:	20.0	
	Staff kitchenette.			:	5.0	
	Caretaker / Cleaner			:	12.0	
	Staff w.c.s/ Disabled toilet			:	8.0	71
5 ANCILLARY	Boiler room and ducts			:	12.0	
	Kitchen (size as existing site)			:	16.0	
	Bins			:	4.0	32
NET TOTAL					839	
6. Circulation at average for single storey of			14 % of net total	:	117.4	
Extra to single storey norm for two stairs				:	26.9	
GROSS FLOOR AREA				:	983	

13.1 *Area analysis*

178

Internal doors: solid core construction.

Wall finishes: generally plaster and emulsion, but with each classroom to have 10 square metres of pin-up board.

Floor finishes: *in corridors*, wet areas and a third of the area of the four classrooms for the youngest children to be hard wearing, easily cleaned and impermeable to water;

in other classroom areas, administration and staffroom areas to use an easily cleaned, fibre based carpet;

in the hall, to use an attractive, hard wearing, non-slip and easily cleaned surface.

Environmental standards were to be as recommended by the DES, and included the following:

Illumination level in classrooms to achieve 300 lux.

Heating to be capable of maintaining a 19 degree temperature difference with one and a half changes per hour.

Daylight factors in classroom areas to be at least two per cent.

The options

Option A: do not move but repair the existing building.

Option B: buy the site being offered and build a single storey structure.

Option C: buy the site being offered and build a two storey structure.

Staffing costs were excluded from the study since these would be similar for all options. Loose furniture was also excluded since the client was not in a position to evaluate his requirements, and this was left as a contingency to be added by the trustees later. It was considered that this cost would be the same for all options and therefore could be ignored. (In any case, if funds were restrictive, the bulk of loose furniture in the existing school could be used in the new accommodation, resulting in only a small extra cost.)

It was argued that if the school moved to a new site, then the improved environment would raise the morale of pupils and staff. It was claimed that this would be reflected in academic standards and that these factors would enable the school to charge higher fees without loss of demand for pupil places. It was considered that school fees could be 3 per cent higher for the new build options.

The financial criteria used to compare these options were their initial costs and their *net present values* (NPVs). The NPVs are the amounts of money which would be required to be invested now in order to pay for costs which occur in the future. The assumptions for calculating these PVs were that the money could be invested at an average annual rate of 12 per cent whilst its purchasing power would be eroded by inflation at an average annual rate of 6 per cent, resulting in a net discount rate of $(12-6)=6$ per cent. The time horizon was forty years. The finance charges of capital and initial costs were calculated at 13 per cent.

Option A
The existing school was surveyed and a programme of repairs was drawn up. This was to be carried out over five years with costs estimated accordingly and discounted back to a present value.

Figure 13.2 shows the figures corresponding to each option.

Option A	Annual cost (where applicable)	Present value
	£	£
Five year programme of repairs		(90,000)
Fees at 6 per cent		(5,400)
Financing costs of above items		(27,600)
Ongoing routine maintenance		(45,000)
Energy costs	(3,300)	(49,700)
Insurance	(750)	(11,300)
Rates	(5,400)	(81,300)
Cleaning and caretaking	(8,800)	(132,400)
School fees (£1,600 × 180)	288,000	4,334,400
	NPV	3,891,700

Say, £3,700,000 to £4,100,000

Option B (956 m²)	Annual cost (where applicable)	Present value
	£	£
Land sale		1,300,000
Land purchase (including land registry fees, stamp duty and land agent's fee at 1.5 per cent)		(600,000)
Capital cost (including fixed furniture at 6 per cent of building cost)		(643,000)

Continued

Continued

Caretaker's flat		(35,000)
Fees at 15 per cent		(101,000)
Financing costs		(54,500)
Maintenance		(35,800)
Energy costs	(2,292)	(34,500)
Insurance	(726)	(10,900)
Rates	(5,394)	(81,200)
Cleaning and caretaking	(8,468)	(127,400)
School fees (1,600 × 1.03 × 180)	296,640	4,464,400
	NPV	4,041,100

Say £3,850,000 to £4,240,000

Option C (983 m²)	Annual cost (where applicable) £	Present value £
Land sale		1,300,000
Land purchase (including land registry fees, stamp duty and land agent's fee at 1.5 per cent)		(600,000)
Capital cost (including fixed furniture at 6 per cent of building cost)		(616,000)
Caretaker's flat		(35,000)
Fees at 15 per cent		(97,000)
Financing costs		(52,400)
Maintenance		(35,800)
Energy costs	(2,244)	(33,800)
Insurance	(692)	(10,400)
Rates	(5,394)	(81,200)
Cleaning and caretaking	(8,578)	(129,100)
School fees (£1,600 × 1.03 × 180)	296,640	4,464,400)
	NPV	4,073,700

Say £3,880,000 to £4,270,000

Note that the gross floor area for option C is slightly higher than for option B because stairs serve the upper floors. The net or teaching floor area can be assumed to be the same.

13.2 *Comparison of options for primary school*

Conclusion

The option with the highest NPV was recommended, reflecting a preference to choose the option with the highest value over the life cycle cost, namely option C. This study of a relatively modest proposal was prepared for a client in the private sector. It was therefore not as broad in scope as studies carried out on large projects or as those often conducted on public sector projects.

index

Index

Weight, DH 78n, 109n
Wood-Robinson, M 78n

Yardsticks 18

Years' purchase 38
Yield 30, 41, 122

Zones 99–102 passim